Social Media Marketing Mastery 2019

3 BOOKS IN 1

How to Build a Brand and Become an Expert Influencer Using Facebook, Twitter, Youtube & Instagram-Top Digital Networking & Personal Branding Strategies

Robert Miller

BOOKS INCLUDED:

Social Media Marketing 2019: *How to Become an Influencer Of Millions On Facebook, Twitter, Youtube & Instagram While Advertising & Building Your Personal Brand*

Social Media Marketing 2019: *The Power of Instagram Marketing - How to Win Followers & Influence Millions Online Using Highly Effective Personal Branding & Digital Networking Strategies*

Social Media Marketing 2019: *How to Brand Yourself Online Through Facebook, Twitter, YouTube & Instagram - Highly Effective Strategies for Digital Networking, Personal Branding, and Online Influence*

Social Media Marketing 2019

How to Become an Influencer of Millions on Facebook, Twitter, YouTube & Instagram While Advertising & Building Your Personal Brand

Robert Miller

Table of Contents

Introduction

Congratulations on getting a copy of *Social Media Marketing 2019: How to Become an Influencer of Millions on Facebook, Twitter, Youtube & Instagram While Advertising & Building Your Personal Brand.*

The influx of social media platforms over the past 10 years is the greatest boon to marketing since the creation of the internet. While there is undeniably money to be made from social media marketing, the shear amount of competition makes getting started successfully more difficult than it would otherwise be.

That's why this book was created, to provide you with the tools you need to get started off on the right foot. The following chapters will discuss how to do just that, starting with an overview of just what makes social media so important in 2019. Next, you will find a detailed breakdown of many of the social media trends you can expect from 2019 and beyond. You will then find an overview of the social media platforms you should get started on as well as how to choose the best starter option for your brand.

From there, you will find chapters dedicated to paid and free marketing strategies for Facebook, Instagram, YouTube, and Twitter. You will find plenty of suggestions for squeezing as many followers and pageviews as possible out of your chosen platform before learning about the paid options and how to best put them to work for you. Finally, you will find plenty of tips and tricks to ensure your content stands out from the pack.

There are plenty of books on this subject on the market, thanks again for choosing this one! Every effort was made to ensure it is full of as much useful information as possible, please enjoy!

Chapter 1: Social Media's Importance

Let's keep this as simple as possible: your business needs an online presence, and a run of the mill website unfortunately just isn't good enough anymore. In 2019 it doesn't matter what type of business you have, if you don't have a social media presence then you are missing out on free marketing. It is an essential part of any business strategy, and if it's not yet a part of yours, now is the time. While there are a lot of people out there who don't use social media, that number gets smaller and smaller every single day, as more and more people sign up for an account.

The past decade, the landscape of the internet has changed drastically, and most of this change is thanks to social media. As a result, it has become a tool for brands and businesses, opening doors to changing your relationship with the public, engage with your base, and increasing sales.

Every small business starts by, among other things, focusing on getting their first customers. Online businesses often target online shoppers, especially those connected via smartphones and other devices. Others rely on traditional forms of advertising like coupon mailers and print ads. However, while these strategies of hoping customers will find business may work, it is advisable to adapt marketing strategies that will prove successful in the long run. For instance, digital marketing enables businesses of all sizes to reach huge online audiences in a measurable and cost effective manner.

Do keep this in mind: businesses can do well without social media. They can make a profit, and break even. But if you want to continue growing, if you want to constantly be improving sales and making more money, if you want to improve your relationship with your customers and engage with them while at the same time not spending too much money, social media is a great way to do this.

Also, don't forget as more and more of the world gets in social media, more and more people will expect to be able to find their favorite businesses and brands online. They want to communicate with you, to know about their product, and they want to know that you care. Making your customers feel connected to you will help your profits go up because they will feel connected to the product they are buying.

Getting into social media marketing can be tough, and overwhelming. It can feel like a huge, giant project, and often business owners, because of this feeling, decide that it's not worth it. But it is. It is 100 percent worth it as you will be able to more easily interact with prospective clients and find out exactly what they are searching for.

Digital marketing methods are also much cheaper compared to traditional marketing means which enables you to reach a much larger audience at very low costs. You also get to track responses to your marketing efforts which in essence enables you to find out what is working and what you can improve on.

Helps your brand: As you know, your brand is the most valuable thing in your business. Every business is fighting to increase or maintain the visibility of their brand. With a strong brand, you have an edge over your competition. Customers are drawn and tend to be more loyal towards popular brands. With social media, you have an affordable digital marketing method for syndicating content and increasing your business' visibility.

You first come up with a great strategy for social media and engage with a wide audience of potential customers. The social media profiles for your business need to be complete and optimized in order to attract your targeted audience. The best way for increasing brand awareness is through generating content. You must publish posts on the regular and invite people to engage with your content. The "likes" and "shares" will introduce your business to new audiences who will potentially become your customers. The following are some things you can expect social media to do to help you increase brand awareness.

Help you to create visual content: People are more likely to share content that has an image as opposed to text only. So, ensure that you put high quality images in your content.

Showcase your personality: it's important to let your charisma shine through. If you deliver the message in a fun and personable way, people subconsciously drop their guards, and it endears your business to them.

Marketing pays real dividends: Marketing is viewed largely as an expense even though in essence it is an investment. It is a crucial activity especially when it comes to attracting the attention of new customers and prospective clients. You are able to develop services and products demand and eventually turn prospective customers into actual customers. Expanding your social media marketing channels means having a presence in as many media platforms as possible. The more popular ones include Twitter, Facebook, Instagram and YouTube all of which are discussed in detail in later chapters

Improve search engine visibility: Every business wants to be able to increase the amount of user engagement and traffic that they have. But is it really possible to do all of this if your potential customers aren't even able to find you when they go online? There are a number of ways that you are able to increase the potential customers to your site, but having a good social media profile can help you dominate those first search result pages in a natural and organic way, and this in turn, increases the profits that you earn.

When you are thinking about this, you can consider the fact that millennials already spend a ton of time on social platforms, and having your own is going to increase the value of your company more than ever. It cannot only help you to generate more business and profits for yourself, but it can also stop some of the brand negativity it takes to reach top positions.

It acts as the mouthpiece for your company: Whether you have been in the industry for a long time, or you are just starting out, having a positive word of mouth for your business will help you to gain more customers and keep your business running. Social media marketing can be a great way to help you as a business owner interact with your customers and generate positive buzz via word of mouth. You can use it to talk about policies in the company, team activities, new launches, and any other information that is needed for the business.

Social networking online can really help your business because you are given a chance to build up a narrative that you can use to capture the interest of your customers. Each piece of content you created can then be curated in such a way that it shares the values and ethics of the company, along with the product, promoting your business on both ends.

Essential social media marketing plan campaign tools

While a successful social media marketing campaign can bring with it a wide variety of potential benefits, it can only do so if you go into it with the right tools from the start.

A good plan: One of the things that you really need to have is a plan that will support your brand and efforts for many years to come. Such a plan will keep you on track and help you to achieve your marketing ambitions. The plan does not need to be as elaborate as a scientific manual. However, it should be clearly written with a well-defined path and exact steps that need to be taken in order to achieve your business's overall aim. If this plan and strategy are then communicated to your team, then your whole business will soon start reaping the dividends of your extensive and elaborate plans. Likewise, if you are working all alone then having clearly defined goals will make it much more likely that you actually reach them.

An excellent product or service: Any social media marketing or advertising campaigns will not bear fruit if you do not have an excellent product or service to offer your future customers. Excellent products or services are those that solve a problem your customers have while at the same time providing a lasting solution. To achieve this you will need to listen to your customers and take their opinions into consideration.

A presentable brand: Having a professional brand is absolutely essential for your success. A brand is much more than just your company's logo. It entails a lot more including what people get to hear and talk about as well as what they feel and think about your business. Make sure that you put together a budget that will support your efforts in building a powerful brand that will stand out from the crowd.

An excellent pitch: As a business owner, you can expect numerous individuals to ask you over and over again about your business and your products. You need to be ready with quality, interesting answers that will intrigue them. Avoid making the mistake of replying with long, boring answers that will drive your potential customers away. Prepare a pitch and make it interesting, fun, and exciting. Then make sure that you are able to deliver it anytime anyone asks about your business regardless of what online setting you find yourself in

Understand ROI: One of the biggest misconceptions that many business leaders will have about Return on Investment (ROI), is that it pertains to revenue generating actions. Unfortunately, this is far from the truth. ROI pertains mostly to the brand building methods that are more profitable in the long run than the conversion of actual sales due to the ad campaign. Social media is about the process of building customer conversation, and connectivity. It is about using social media outlets to reach those that are not familiar with your brand and helping them to understand your passions as a company.

There are a few metrics that need to be monitored to examine the impact your social media account is having on your ROI. These include:

- Lifetime Value
- Churn
- The overall cost of operation

Lifetime value is a measurement that will calculate the frequency as well as the annual total of purchases for each customer prior to the ad campaign and after the ad campaign. By using the lifetime value as a calculative measure for the ROI you are setting a baseline for the impact that the social media ad campaign is having on your bottom line.

To understand how social media is hurting or improving your customers' loyalty you can check the churn. The churn will tell you how many customers you have gained or lost, as well as the volume by which it went up or down. Next, you will work towards understanding the concept that a dollar that is saved is also a dollar that is earned. It can be quite difficult to measure the ROI of your social media account, however, you can measure the social media's impact that has taken place on the brand's equity, as well as the benefit of the bottom line.

Chapter 2: 2019 Trends

Social media is here to stay, and it looks like it is only going to become even more influential as it continues to evolve and change quickly to keep up with the ever growing demands of society. Experiences will only become more interactive, immersive and influential, and for a business to survive, it must be leveraging the social media experience at every opportunity. Social media marketing is here to stay.

Innovation in marketing in this era is essential. As a business owner, you need to keep yourself updated with some of the latest trends in marketing and advertising. There are quite a number of innovations that will be adapted in 2019 that will help to take your business to the next level. For the foreseeable future at least, especially these are a few important trends to keep tabs on including the increasing importance of influencers, VR and AR, sales enablement, artificial intelligence, and even more personalized content.

Influencers will be more important than ever

Come the year 2020, influencer marketing is projected to become and industry capable of raking in 10 billion dollars. Given the rise of influencers across every social media platform channel, this is a very real possibility. Gen Z and the millennials have also embraced influencers in their lives, welcoming the power of their social media storytelling, even using that power to help them make decisions on whether they should purchase a product or service. Watching unboxing videos or product reviews on YouTube where an influencer shows off the latest gadget, beauty product, fashion haul, etc., has created a unique and immersive experience.

The following are some of the reasons why marketers are turning to influencers to promote their products:

- *Influencers have earned their followers' trust:* someone is more likely to buy a product when it's recommended by a person that they trust. An influencer has already earned the trust of their followers and it puts them in a better position to recommend products.
- *Influencers give you access to a targeted audience:* promoting a product to a small niche-audience is much more rewarding than blasting an ad to a crowd who couldn't care less about your product. When you use an influencer, you gain access to a laser-targeted audience who are likely to purchase your product.
- *Relatively inexpensive:* influencers are very affordable as long as you don't go for Hollywood stars and athletes. For instance, micro influencers charge between $200 and $250 for a post, which is a reasonable price considering they are exposing you to thousands of their targeted followers. Some marketers seem to be of the notion that influencers are too expensive when it isn't the case at all.
- *Boosts SEO:* another method of getting strong backlinks to your site is by leveraging social media influencers. When influencers link to your site, it boosts both your domain authority and page authority, which in turn improves SEO.

While it seems as though influencers hit the mainstream relatively recently, it is already an established part of the status quo to the point that well-known influencers are already making thousands of dollars, if not more, for sponsorships and brand associations. As such, if you have already heard of an influencer then odds are you likely can't afford them if you are just starting out. This is where the latest tier of influencers, known as micro-influencers come into play.

Micro-influencers, as the name implies, do not have followers in the millions, or even in the hundreds of thousands, instead, they typically have around 50,000 followers or less. While the numbers may not be as high, the followers that these micro-influencers have tend to be far more committed than those of their larger peers, to the point that a food brand would likely see a better ROI working with a food blogger with 50,000 followers and a reasonable budget than a more famous alternative whose price is 10 times as high.

The trend of drilling down to find even smaller, and more dedicated, followings is only going to increase in 2019 to the point where nano-influencers, those with a max of 10,000 dedicated followers, are going to start becoming relevant as well. Those who are members of these smaller communities tend to be the most dedicated at all which means that if their favorite nano-influencer recommends your brand the conversion rate is typically greater than 50 percent. As these individuals can often be bought for $100 or some free merchandise, the ROI on this type of social media marketing is only going to continue to increase.

What's more, many of these individuals are completely new to the business which means that they are anxious to form long-term partnerships. As they don't require a large budget to work with, you may be in a place to easily lock an individual down early if you find someone that is clearly going to a big hit once they become a bit more well-known.

Virtual and augmented reality: The term Omni-channel originated around customers in order to describe marketing strategies that exist outside the travel and retail sectors. Omni simply means every kind, all, or the whole. Therefore, Omni-channel marketing refers to reaching out to customers and interacting with them across all possible communication channels, though these days there is an increasing focus on AR and VR. Even then, a focus should be placed on budgets so that only the most effective channels are selected.

Businesses are now using mobile cameras in order to improve customer experience. Through both virtual reality and augmented reality, you can promote brand engagement and also make the pre-purchase decision much easier for your customers. The process will almost bring your products to life. Your customers will be able to make life much easier and better for your customers.

Increased sales enablement: Social media is already well-known for being able to make the product discovery phase of shopping easier than ever before. It allows brands to promote their products through a virtually endless array of channels that make it as easy for the customer to make a purchase as possible. This is only going to continue into 2019 as every social media platform continues to trend towards improved enablement of sales in the business funnel.

According to a recent study of 2018 internet trends, more than 50 percent of those polled had discovered a product via social media that they then subsequently purchased within the past month. Of the social media platforms discussed in this book, Instagram is the leading platform that led to these types of conversions.

Now is the time to take advantage of this trend and get your brand into a position where it can benefit by improving your social strategy. This also means that you will not always need a sales pitch in all of your messaging if you want people to trust you. Instead, social media is making it easier than ever to help you to tell your story and to improve your odds of consideration.

Artificial intelligence: Automated bots have already begun to show up as part of the customer service options for many brands and this type of artificial intelligence is only going to become more common across all social media platforms in 2019. Social media has made it easier than ever for customers to talk to their favorite brands directly and, while this is great in some respects, it also means general expectations for support response times are decreasing.

Chatbots are a natural way to solve this problem while still providing what appears to be personalized customer service. While not all customers are going to be comfortable using chatbots at first, as the adoption rate improves more and more people are sure to get on board once they interact with a few of then and understand their limitations.

What's even better is that the influx of interest in this type of technology means that the responses that these customer service programs can provide are going to become more and more real to the point that most people won't know when they are texting with a real person and when they are talking to a machine. This can take several forms including giving them more personality or simply predicting the types of questions customers are going to ask and writing more detailed responses to cater to every possibility.

AI is also becoming increasing prevalent when it comes to automated messaging to common voiced questions. More and more brands are staffing their customer service centers with messaging that can keep the customer satisfied while at the same time saving money and preventing a person from having to answer the same question dozens of times per day.

Increase emphasis on stories: Stories are becoming more prevalent for brands of all shapes and sizes. This type of vertical, visual content started on Snapchat and was eventually copied by Instagram before moving to Facebook, YouTube and beyond where it has taken the mainstream by storm and will continue to do so into 2019. As of January 2019, there are more than 500 million people consuming stories in one form or another each day which means that harnessing this power effectively is key to remaining relevant in 2019.

Stories are so effective because they allow brands to spark real conversations with their followers in a way that feels organic. As the algorithms that power modern social media platforms become more and more decisive it is no longer enough for brands to encourage followers to like, follow and subscribe, more personal connections are needed. This is going to become increasingly important in 2019 as additional new types of engagement come to the fore, leaving older options left in the dust.

Micro-moment marketing: Micro-moment marketing is all about the changing nature of consumer behavior in the context of their own digital (especially mobile-based) behavior as well as the fact that they are facing information overload as they spend so much time online.

It's based on the idea that consumers today can basically access the "best" of anything in the space of a few seconds--and some 96 percent of consumers will be doing this with their smartphones in the space of a few seconds.

The challenge that this poses to brands and marketers is that now they must be able to essentially "find" their customer in the space of these few moments without having any relevant information about them ahead of time. Thus, businesses must be able to offer more in the way of "one-touch" offerings to accommodate this behavior, build brand loyalty, and stay ahead of their competition.

Traditional marketing is an interruption – if you come "at" them, they're going to be annoyed. But they can choose to come and find you when they need something. So, in the sense that consumers have so many choices available "in the moment," the marketing game has changed. Highly personalized "smart content" that's focused on relationship-building is one response to this, essentially finding a way to address very specific buyer personas. This can be tailored towards a specific characteristic of a demographic, including age, location or even what point in the buyer's journey a person is.

Chapter 3: Primary Social Media Platforms

A big part of successfully rolling out your own social media marketing plan is targeting the right platforms to ensure that your efforts are reaching the greatest portion of your audience as possible. While you will likely want to end up expanding to all of the platforms outlined below, you will want to put your efforts into getting one up and running at a time to ensure you can start seeing the benefits of your efforts as soon as possible.

Factors to consider when choosing a starter social media platform for business purposes include

Cost: The first social network that you work with should be one that has plenty of free advertising options as you will want to avoid paid options until you get a better idea of what works and what does not. If you have to pay to be on social media, then it may not be worth it in the short-term. There are lots of free advertising options for each of the major social media platforms, it is just a matter of determining which seem as though they will work most effectively for you.

Suitability for small businesses: It is important to choose an option that you know you can keep up in the long-term. Starting a social media profile and then leaving it untended is worse than not having one at all. Not having an account is a choice that can be defended, having a poorly curated account shows that you don't care about your online appearance and can be enough turn some people away right from the start.

Popularity for your niche: There are two types of thought when it comes to the best type of platform to choose. You can either choose one that is popular with other small businesses in your niche, or you can go the other way and go with a lesser picked option. On one hand, you know that people interested in your niche will be on the platform and looking to engage in content, but you risk being lost in the crowd. On the other hand, you will be able to stand out more easily, but you don't know if there is going to be anybody looking. Neither option is superior to the other as long as you know what you are getting into.

Ease of use: It is important to have an idea of what type of content you are going to be creating the most of as you will want to ensure the primary platform you choose is one that you won't have to fight with every time you want to create a post.

Advanced features: You are able to achieve a lot more an engage your customers and followers better on social networks with advanced features.

Geographic targeting: Most small businesses have a local focus so the ability to target a specific niche of the market or particular geographic area adds lots of value.

Age: There are some social networks that are more popular with certain age groups. For instance, Instagram is more popular with millennials while Facebook is suitable for people of all ages.

Facebook

Facebook is an incredibly powerful marketing tool that is essential for any successful small business owner to take advantage of. Businesses who are not actively using Facebook in some way, shape, or form are robbing themselves of untold profits. It continues to be one of the leading social networking platforms, making it a huge tool for accessing your target market and increasing your sales.

Here are some of the reasons why you need to be taking advantage of Facebook for marketing your business:

A massive number of active users: The sheer size of Facebook's active users alone should be enough to encourage any company to lay down roots on the Facebook network. Facebook has more than 1 billion active users visiting its site on a daily basis, and more than 2 billion active monthly visitors. This means that on a daily basis you are tapping into a market that accounts for 1/7 to 2/7 of the entire global population. The reach is massive, making it a highly valuable tool for marketers to use.

Evenly split demographics: Every network has its demographic audience, but almost none stack up to Facebook. Facebook is unique in a sense that it has a very evenly split demographic. It's users are a strong balance of men and women from nations all across the globe. With this balance, that means it is almost a given that your niche will be hanging out on Facebook ready to consume your content!

Global network: Facebook has a strong North American presence, but it actually has an incredibly strong international presence as well. India, Brazil, and Indonesia account for a great deal of the active daily audience after the US. This means that you can expand your target audience far beyond the core and capitalize in a far bigger way using Facebook.

Language translation: Something that regularly holds people back from being able to conduct business across borders is language barriers. Not being able to communicate with international audience's in a language they understand can ultimately hinder your ability to sell overseas. Not anymore, though! Facebook has more than 70 translations available on its platform meaning that users from all around the world can read your page and purchase anything you may be selling.

Instagram

Instagram is extremely popular with people under 30, them making up 59 percent of the platform, and people under 25 use Instagram for an average of 32 minutes a day. In terms of teenagers, 72 percent of them use Instagram every day, second only to Snapchat, and since Instagram has put in a story option similar to Snapchat's formula, that number is getting higher. This is an extremely valuable tool if your product is more aimed towards that generation.

If you want your business to be picked up internationally, 80 percent of Instagram users are outside the US. This is especially valuable if your product is something that can be ordered or used online, like a course or a blog. If you're located in a tourist town, this is also a thing to consider.

YouTube

YouTube originally made itself known with cat videos and wacky, obscure content, but now it is the world's second largest search engine, second only to Google. There are over a billion users, nearly a third of everyone on the internet, and every day billions of hours of video are consume. YouTube can be navigated in 76 different languages, that is 95 percent of everyone on the internet, and it is the second most visited website in the world.

Google prioritizes video content in its search results, especially video coming from YouTube. Website pages with video are 53 times more likely to rank highly on Google searches. It is plain to see why YouTube is a cut above other video sharing services with those statistics alone. If you want to get your name out there, it will go a long way towards helping you. However, why should you care about getting your name out there?

If you are a creative person, the answer might seem obvious, because you enjoy creating content whether makeup tutorials or video game streams and sharing it. But, if you are a business, the answer might be more difficult to see initially.
The beauty of YouTube for business is that it gives you a chance to get personal with your audience and gain their trust. For instance, say you run a small physical therapy business. You could produce videos on how to do a variety of exercises, thus setting yourself up as an authority on the matter and hopefully pulling in more customers.

It may seem counter-intuitive to teach your audience what you want them to buy from you, but once they start learning from you, they will trust you and see the value you offer, making them more likely to use your business in the future.
YouTube also allows you to interact with your audience and customers. Try asking them questions in your videos, or if you notice people asking the same question frequently, you can make a video answering that question.

You can comment on other people's channels, getting your name across their screen, which they will hopefully click if you are compelling. If you build that bond viewers become loyal, and it will also help you better understand who your audience is, thus making you able to market yourself better.

Creating your own YouTube channel is as easy as creating a Google account which is to say that if you already have some type of Google account then you already have a YouTube channel waiting for you. To activate it, all you need to do is to log into your Google account as normal before heading to YouTube.com and looking for the choice listed as My Channel. Clicking on this option will allow you to name your page and doing so will officially create it. When it comes to choosing a name for your page, the first thing you are going to want to do is to determine what type of content you are going to create and then choose a name that is relevant to that type of content. You will also then want to add in keywords and phrases that are related to the type of content you ultimately decided to produce.

Decide on content: If you aren't interested in creating content that personally means something to you, and are instead more concerned with appealing to the widest variety of advertisers, then you are likely going to want to consider creating product review videos. Essentially, these are going to be short (3 minutes maximum) videos that break down a product's relative strengths and weakness and they are extremely popular and can be targeted at a specific audience with ease. As such, you are going to want to choose an audience that is specific enough that it can easily be targeted by marketers.

This means you are going to want to focus on a segment of the market that has disposable income and a hobby or interest that is never going to be at a loss for new products. The best case scenario is to find a niche with a wide margin of product prices as you are going to have to purchase every item you review, at least until you start getting some clout in your niche. If you can make your channel all about reviewing the cheap end of an expensive hobby, then you can target those types of advertisers looking to pull in the big fish without spending an arm and a leg yourself.

Add content: After you have created your account and determined what types of videos you are going to be creating on the regular, the next thing you are going to need to do is to actually start creating content. If you are unsure of what a good product review video looks like, simply search for a review of a product you are already familiar with so you know what is being discussed.

When it comes to ensuring views, the best way to do so is to encourage viewers to subscribe to your channel and the best way to do that is to post quality content on a regular basis. You are going to want to start off by posting between 15 and 20 videos and then post at least two new entries every week. This way you will provide potential subscribers with enough relevant and quality content that they feel justified in being notified each time you post a new video. Additionally, you will want to ensure that each video is labeled and tagged appropriately so that those in your chosen niche will be able to find it with even the most generic niche related searches.

Profit: Once your new videos are regularly generating at least 1,000 views per video you will know that you have enough of a subscriber base to begin to successfully monetize your page. Luckily, the key to doing so is already built into your channel through what is known as the monetization tab. This tab can be found in the options menu and it will let YouTube start placing relevant advertisements before your videos. You will also want to connect your channel to Google AdSense which, in turn, will turn on various advertisements based on each viewer's browser history. More information on AdSense can be found at Google.com/AdSense.

Both of these types of advertisements will start out with a pay per click structure, though if you reach enough subscribers you will eventually gain access to pay per view advertisements as well. If you plan on making money in this fashion it is important to never use copyrighted material in your videos. A pay per click structure typically pays out 20 cents per click, with 1,000 views being enough to assume 10 people will actually click on the advertisement in question. If you gain enough of a following to qualify for pay per view type ads, then you can expect to make roughly $3 for every 1,000 views the ad receives.

This is why YouTube affiliate marketing is such a numbers game as it is practically impossible to create only a small number of videos that return the type of views that are required to generate anything remotely resembling a reliable revenue stream. Instead, you are going to want to create as many videos as possible, especially as your subscriber base initially takes off. This is because the internet is inherently fickle, which means you will want to capitalize on any moments of popularity that you do experience as you never know how long they are going to last.

Twitter

This platform is great for some businesses but not for all. This is why you need to understand the different types of social media. Twitter is awesome for mini posts and sharing links to blog posts and articles. The platform is designed to allow users to post short messages known as tweets. However, you can also post links, images, videos, polls, and much more.

Twitter is ideal for businesses that target a tech-savvy audience, elites, intellects who love brief but precise messages and information in bit-sized chunks. Keep in mind that this is the world's third largest social media platform so doing well here can be a huge blessing. As a business owner, you should set up a Twitter business page and start reaching out to customers and other members on the platform. When you do, you will be able to gain a presence and thereby establish a brand identity.

The ideal posts to share include business information, launches and events, time-sensitive updates, shout-outs, and to re-tweet other people's posts. It is advisable to post between one and three times each day to the more than 275 million monthly visitors.

To create an account on Twitter, simply go to the Twitter for Business page and then simply sign up. Once your account is up and running, you should start following major brands, influential individuals, as well as users within your niche. You should also begin posting updates and providing links to useful content and helpful articles. Re-tweeting is also highly advisable so re-tweet any content that you find interesting, catchy, exciting and so on. Remember that there are customers out there who rely on platforms such as Twitter to communicate with brands and receive customer service.

If you have a very visible brand or perhaps you do not own a blog, then you may wish to skip this platform. Please note, however, that there are numerous companies that thrive on this platform. This is because of their unique products and brand as well as a distinct voice. Try and set yourself apart so that you stand out among the rest. Companies thrive on Twitter when they engage their customers and listen as they express themselves and share their concerns.

Chapter 4: Facebook Marketing 2019

How many people do you currently know who are NOT on Facebook? The answer you've most likely given is – no one. Because everyone is on Facebook. Billions of people from around the globe hold a Facebook social media account and that is exactly why existing businesses and prospective businesses should get online and get on Facebook (if they haven't already done so). Not only are those billions of people connected on this social media platform, but they log in multiple times in a day just to either check what's happening or to post an update themselves. For a business, that's almost a billion people a day, multiple times a day who could potentially see your product or service.

With features such as page insights, content, page and ad management, content curation and more, Facebook is a social media marketing goldmine for businesses. And the best part of this is setting up a basic page for a business is free! Some features on Facebook require you to pay a small fee, but the unbeatable low price that the social media platform is quoting is a lot lower than it would cost to market the conventional way.

One of the biggest challenges faced by business users of Facebook and other social media platforms who are using these as marketing tools are getting their followers to become paying customers. Gathering a large following on a Facebook page is one step. The next step is converting those followers into paying customers which can only be done with a lot of patience.

Social media is a constantly changing environment. Information just keeps coming in one after another and it's evident by how quickly items appear on a Facebook newsfeed. When it comes to marketing on social media platforms like Facebook, businesses need to be patient. Remember that it's Facebook, and users lose interest and get distracted quickly. What you need to do as a business is to keep their attention, and hold on to it long enough to change their minds about buying from your business. This chapter will focus on the free opportunities Facebook offers when it comes to advertising

Become an authority

In order to attract the type of readers that are interested in the content you are peddling, the best way to do this reliably is to start posting content on a regular basis and then never stop. During the early days, it is important to keep posting regularly, using appropriate SEO, even if you aren't getting any hits. You are going to need a backlog of content regardless, so keep at it and don't lose faith in the process.

In many situations, the word expert and the word authority are often used interchangeably; this is not the case with sales, however, as being an authority is everything and being an expert is much worse than simply getting second place. In this case, an expert is someone who knows a lot about a certain niche while an authority is the person that all of the experts agree is the first stop for information. To put it another way, authorities aren't authorities because they say they are, they are authorities because when they make declarations in regard to their niche of choice, other people listen.

The benefits of being an authority for your chosen niche are much the same as being an authority in any other situation when you speak, other people listen. This is because those who know you are an authority are naturally going to assume you know what you are talking about for a given situation. It doesn't take much to see how this can translate directly into additional conversions when given a little extra push. If you can reach the status of authority for your niche, then you will be able to set the tone for the niche as a whole, along with legions of fans that will be willing to automatically agree with whatever you say.

During this period, you are going to want to seek out the online spaces that people interested in your niche tend to congregate and become a fixture in them. This means competing blogs, YouTube channels, subreddits, essentially wherever the audience you are targeting goes, they need to see you. During this phase, it is important to only include links to your posts occasionally, as you want people to engage in your content and not get turned off because they think it is a marketing ploy. Instead of focusing on marketing, focus on providing your target audience with useful information and before long they will start seeking you out.

Once your name begins to get out there, you can then move on to capturing the attention of the other experts in the niche. Any expert can offer up their opinion, the authority in a given niche is the one that the other experts seek out as well. This means that you will want to eventually reach out to the creators of the niche blogs you have been frequenting and offer to contribute to their blog. As long as you provide links to your own content which shows you are an expert, many bloggers will be happy to not have to generate a post for once and take you up on your offer. Once your name starts showing up on other niche websites, you know you are one your way to becoming an authority.

Once you start driving traffic to your site directly from competing blogs, the next thing you are going to want to do is to use the outline you wrote when you were becoming an expert and expand it into a full eBook. Writing a 5,000-word book on the niche in question should come easily to you at this point, and you can put the whole thing together by yourself and even post it to the Amazon Kindle Marketplace, all for free. You then give the book away in exchange for signing up for the email newsletter that you will want to set up, in an effort to start collecting information on your readers in an effort to market to them more effectively. The regular visitors to your page are likely to sign up, putting them in the prime spot for the marketing of products targeted to those with a clearly defined group of interests.

Create Facebook Groups

Help your customers: The second type of Facebook groups is dedicated to acquired customers. To build this community, invite people to join the group as soon as they make a purchase. Make customers aware of the existence of the group and that you would like them if they too registered.

Explain how the group works in the "information" section. For example, members can get to know each other, share ideas and strategies and help each other in any way. Be sure to send an email with the link to subscribe to the group and monitor who signs up or not. Do not forget to invite people who have not yet registered several times.

Here are some ways to develop your group on Facebook:

Be generous and promote a "give" policy: For example, offer tips or tricks to use the lesser known features of your product and invite other users to share their findings. You could invite members of your fan group to share tips and tricks with them too.

Be transparent: Respond personally to customer criticism. For example, thank the customer who makes you notice the flaw in your product and respond that you will immediately fix it. It is not necessary to promise discounts or promotions to the disgruntled customer, but it is important to thank him for the report, to apologize and to promise that he will be contacted when the problem is solved.

Be present: Answer questions and comments as soon as possible. If you cannot give an immediate answer, still let your customer know that you will respond quickly.

Be inclusive: Offer group members promotions and offers that are not on the official page. Make your customers feel part of an exclusive club.

Chapter 5: Paid Facebook Marketing

Creating a great campaign with Facebook Ads can seem a little bit overwhelming in the beginning, but there are so many great things that you can do when you utilize all the features that come with it. While you do need to think about the ad itself, you must make sure you understand the platform that you are using. Once you determine who you're trying to target, and you have a good idea of how much you want to spend on the campaign, then it is easier to focus on some of the smaller details.

You need to make sure that from the beginning you set up a budget and a bid strategy for your campaign. Otherwise, you will keep the campaign going way too long and you will end up spending more than you intended. Facebook has made this part easy though with the use of Optimized CPM.

With this kind of tool, you are giving Facebook the permission it needs to bid for ad space based on any goals or constraints that you provide to it. This is often the best way for you, especially as a beginner, to maximize your budget and avoid any overspending. Until you are able to get an idea of how much the ad space costs, and how to best allocate your budget, just stick with the Optimized CPM to get the most out of your campaign.

A Facebook ad campaign has three levels. At the top is the Campaign, then the Ad Set, and then the Ad itself. At the campaign level, you will choose an objective or goal like "Increase Sales" or "Increase Total Likes for my Business Facebook Page." At the Ad Set level, you will set your budget, your schedule, your target audience, and your ad placement. Once you have chosen the parameters of your ad set, you will design your ad or multiple ads to be run with the same ad set. Your ad set may contain one or more ads, and the ads must be individual creations that contain text, video, images, and/or links. Your ad set is what will attract attention to your business or brand and will help you achieve both your short-term and long-term goals.

Facebook Ads vs Boosted Posts: Which Should You Choose?

This question is very common among the admins of Facebook pages. Even if you are new to a page, you are bound to see Facebook's prompt to 'boost a post' and this usually comes in when Facebook detects high activity on a certain post or if its algorithms have found other pages with similar content boosting a certain type of content that matches yours. The ability to boost your post is a very simplified addition to Facebook Ads system. This system is designed to be simple and easy to use even for a non-marketer or advertiser. However, simple doesn't always mean better. Boosted posts come at the cost of significant customization the complete ad system provides.

What have boosted posts on Facebook?

With boosted posts, advertisers have the choice to use a post that has already been posted at any time and promote it. When boosting a post, page admins can choose their target audience, decide on a budget and how long the boosted post should run. This can be done on any post on your page's timeline.

Facebook Ads vs boosted posts: A post that is boosted focuses on increased visibility for that particular post and in an effort to increase engagement as much as possible. Boosted posts are great for brand awareness and an increase in engagement can be value added for social proof. An increase in engagement can also mean a lower CPC (cost-per-click) or CPA (cost-per-acquisition), you also could end up with more results with the same value of the investment.

With Facebook's recent update, you not only can increase engagement for that particular post, but you can also choose the outcome of it- whether you want people to visit your profile more or visit your site. If this is your option, compared to increasing engagement on the post in terms of likes or comments, your ad be visible to people who will most likely end up clicking. This option is available only if your boosted post has a link to it.

Step one – Determine your goals

The first step towards creating an effective ad campaign structure is to set firm and clear goals, and then to allocate each goal to an individual campaign. Then, every ad set and the ad will be oriented towards your chosen objectives - no matter how big or small, how long-term or how short term. For example, your objective may be something like increasing the number of installs your app has, increasing overall traffic to your website, increasing sales of a particular item, or simply to generate more "Likes" for your Facebook business page.

Tip #1: Limit one objective per advertisement, that way you can tailor your audience and budget to achieve maximum value from your ad campaign.

Tip #2: *Get creative! If your objective is to increase Page Likes, consider designing an ad that offers a 10% discount code to anyone who Likes and Follows your business Facebook page. While this would work well for increasing Facebook Page Likes, offering 10% off for a Facebook Like may not generate more website traffic, since your website is not directly involved. This is why we recommend limiting your objectives to one objective per ad.*

Step two - Define your audience

The second step is to allocate your ad sets to the audiences you most want to target. One ad set might be aimed at Men, age 18 to 24, while another ad set might aim at Women, age 18 to 24. It is important to allocate different ad sets to different audiences so that your ad sets do not end up competing with one other. It also important to keep your target audience in mind when designing each ad set. Men may be more likely to stop and look at an ad that includes a scantily-clad model in it, but most women will probably scroll right past - or worse, they may block the ad.

The proper ad campaign structure is crucial for any business, small or large, and any brand, whether that brand supports a single product or many products. With a well-formed, thoughtfully-designed ad campaign, your company could see an increase in website or social media traffic, an increase in profits, improved brand recognition, and so much more!

An effective campaign structure is the first step in a successful ad campaign, as it will help you to set specific goals for specific campaigns, measure the results of those campaigns, discover which campaigns are working and which are not, and allocate your budget in the most effective way possible. It will also help you to create multiple ad sets for multiple audiences so that you can determine who is most likely to generate business for your company or brand. Through variations in image, text, links, and videos, a properly structured campaign will even allow you to see what types of ads are having the biggest impact on your audience.

Facebook can help you build your audience. Facebook Ads Manager separates the different types of audience into three categories: Core Audiences, Custom Audiences, and Lookalike Audiences.

Facebook Ads Manager allows you to manually narrow down your Core Audience by the following factors:

Location: There are four options which shape the scope of your audience targeting.

- Everyone (for everyone in a given area)
- Locals (those that claim the area as "home")
- New Residents (those who have recently updated the area as "home")
- Visitors (those have recently "checked in" to this location, or nearby locations)

The "given area" can be the narrowed down by your zip code, and can even include neighboring zip codes if you are looking for a broader reach. The location of your audience is important to consider, as not every business is looking for tourists and not every business is looking for locals. For example a hotel would want to target visitors and tourists, whereas a bakery will want to target local residents.

Consider location carefully before making a decision about which locations or areas to include in your campaign. If you are advertising a product that can be shipped outside of your state, or outside of your country, then you will want the location to be very broad. However, if you are advertising a specific service, you may only want to advertise in the area that you are willing to provide this service.

For example: If your business is a Maid service, you may only want to advertise within the sixty square miles of your home or business. It probably would not make sense to advertise your Maid service hundreds of miles away.

Demographics: Facebook allows marketers to target specific age ranges, specific genders, and specific spoken languages.

- Age Ranges: while a hotel would want to target all age ranges, a tattoo parlor may only want to target people under the age of 40. Be sure to choose an age range that suits your product or business.
- Genders: again, while a hotel may want to target all genders, a hair salon may only want to target women. 90% of the time, you will want to target both men and women, so consider very carefully before choosing to exclude either gender.
- Languages: if the staff at your business speak more than language, it is important to advertise this. For example, if your business is based in Southwest Arizona, and you (or a staff member) are fluent in Spanish, as well as English, advertise to both English-speaking and Spanish-speaking customers.

Interest: Targeting by interest allows marketers to reach people based on what they have listed as their interests and activities on their Facebook profile, the posts and comments that they have "liked" on Facebook, and the posts and comments that they have created. For example, if your business makes customized dog collars, Facebook Ads Manager will target users who have dogs, follow dog- or pet-related pages, or have dogs listed as an interest in their profile.

Behavior: Targeting by behavior allows marketers to reach people based on what they buy, what kinds of devices they use, whether they are using a desktop to access Facebook or a mobile phone, and other similar factors. For example, if you are advertising your new iPhone app, Facebook Ads Manager will target users who access Facebook via their iPhone or other Apple-branded product. After all, iPhone apps are only available for iPhones and cannot be used across other mobile phone platforms or operating systems.

Connections: Targeting by connections allows marketers to select their audience based on their connections to pages, apps, or events. It also allows you to target the friends of people connected to pages and apps. Example: if your business is a bakery, you can target audience members that have liked other bakeries in your area.

Audience size: Be aware that with every factor you use to narrow your audience, your target audience may become very small. This is where it is important to consider including zip codes beyond your own. Be sure to pay close attention to the Audience Size Indicator provided by the Facebook Ads Manager, to make sure you are not spending a large amount of your budget on a very small or narrow audience.

Custom Audiences: Custom Audiences are audiences built on your own data, as opposed to the Core Audiences which are based solely on Facebook's data. Custom Audience sources can come from data files (from your Point of Sale system, your email lists, or your client database). Custom Audience sources can also come from website data (data collected from your company's website), mobile app data (data collected from your company's mobile apps), or Facebook data (data collected from people's interactions with your Facebook page, ads, and videos).

Make sure your data sources coincide with your goals. For example, if you are looking to drive up sales and increase revenue, you should be targeting frequent shoppers and high-value clients.

It is also important to ensure that the proper devices have been targeted. For instance, if your audience tends to shop more via mobile phone, your targeting should reflect this. Use complete and up-to-date data for the best results. If you are using an email list to generate your audience, make sure that email list is up-to-date, and not riddled with old email accounts that are no longer in use. Using old information will only result in your ad budget being wasted.

You can also use your Custom Audience data to target customers based on their previous interactions with your business.

- If a customer has made a prior purchase, you could advertise complementary products.
- Re-market old products to members of your audience that have already encountered your message.
- Use Custom Audiences to upsell.
- Use Custom Audiences to show new customers that they have friends or connections that like your business or use your product or service.

Facebook uses a security process called "data hashing," which heavily encrypts your data. Facebook's data hashing has been reviewed by an independent third party, Pricewaterhouse Coopers, and they have confirmed that your data is secure - from the implementation of your data to the storage of your data. So, you need not worry that the audience information you share or the payment information you provide is vulnerable to cyber threats. While no system can ever be 100% secure, Facebook's data hashing severely limits the actual threat to your information.

Lookalike audiences: Lookalike Audiences are people who have similar online traits to your current customer base. There are three types of Lookalike Audiences: Value-Based Lookalikes, International Lookalikes, and Multi-Country Lookalikes.

Value-Based Lookalikes: When creating a Custom Audience, you can create a customer value file which will help you find new customers who are similar to your highest spending, or high-value, clients. For example, if many of your high-value clients are considered "upper class," you may want to target an audience that frequents expensive local restaurants or local golf clubs. When creating a Value-Based Lookalike audience in Facebook Ads Manager, it is important that stereotypes exist for a reason, and stereotypes can definitely be used to your advantage in terms of marketing and advertising.

International Lookalikes: For a company to expand across the globe, Lookalike Audiences can target those who most resemble your customer base in any country - not just in one particular region. This is especially valuable if your company provides goods with international shipping options.

Multi-Country Lookalikes: Target a region, such as Europe or North America, and market across multiple countries at the same time. This is especially valuable if your business is located near another country. For example, if your business is located in northern Michigan, targeting audience members in Canada may be beneficial, as they may be willing to cross the border if your services are of particular interest to them.

To create a Lookalike Audience, you must first create a Seed Audience. This is a sample of at least one hundred of your best customers - those that are heavily engaged in your online content, or those who make the largest or most valuable purchases. The more people in your Seed Audience, the better Facebook can help find Lookalike audiences.

Seed Audiences can be created from Custom Audiences, from data collected from your website and/or mobile app, and from the data collected from your Facebook pages. When creating a Lookalike Audience, it is important to consider your end goal. Are you looking for a new audience similar to your existing audience? Or are you looking to broaden your overall reach by adding to your existing audience?

When choosing your audience size in the Facebook Ads Manager, know that if your audience size is closer to "one," you will get a smaller but more similar audience to your current seed audience. If the audience size number in the Facebook Ads Manager is closer to "ten," you will get a larger, broader audience, but it may contain fewer (if any) similarities to that of your seed audience.

Once you have saved your Core Audience, Custom Audience, and Lookalike Audience, you can access them for future ad campaigns in the Facebook Ads Manager. You can also alter their parameters in the event that overlap between your various audiences lowers the delivery of your ad sets.

If you have multiple ad sets targeting similar audiences during the same period of time, then your ad sets might end up competing with each other in the ad auction. This can drive up prices and lead to an inefficient or ineffective use of your budget.

Know your budget: When you allocate your audience, you will also be at the point in ad set design where you will get to determine how to allocate your budget and the different aspects of budgeting you will need to keep in mind. The first two aspects of budgeting to consider are Daily Budget and Lifetime Budget.

- Daily Budget: the amount you are willing to spend on an ad set per day.

- Lifetime Budget: the amount you are willing to spend on an ad set in total.

Facebook Ads Manager also provides two specialty buying options, Reach & Frequency and Target Rating Points.

- **Reach & Frequency:** This specialty buying option is ideal if your campaign needs to target more than 200,000 people. It provides controlled ad delivery at a locked price. For more information, visit the Facebook Business page at https://www.facebook.com/business/learn/facebook-reach-and-frequency-buying

- **Target Rating Points:** This specialty buying option allows you to purchase video ads on Facebook, much like you would if you were purchasing television ads on a national network. For more information, visit the Facebook Business FAQ page at https://www.facebook.com/business/help/5189937282 99293

Facebook ad campaigns can cost you as little as $5.00 a week, or as much as $50,000 a week. This aspect is highly customizable. Once a budget is set, the Facebook Ad Manager will automatically calculate the "audience reach," based on your budget and the length of time you have chosen to run the campaign. If you want your ad to reach a wider audience, you can either increase your budget or reduce the length of your ad campaign.

The Ads Manager will also calculate the cost per result for you. If you, or your client, want to set a budget based on the cost per result (instead of a budget based on the campaign as a whole), this calculation is the one you will need to look at most closely.

In addition, Facebook Ads Manager allows to tailor your budget even further in the following ways:

- Campaign Spending Limit: This parameter allows you to set the maximum amount you are willing to spend on the advertising campaign in question. This is your overall budget for a SINGLE ad.
- Account Spending Limit: This parameter allows you to set a maximum amount you are willing to spend on ALL of your campaigns, not just one particular ad.

Given the specific requirements of your advertising campaign, like the budget, bid, or targeted audience, the Ads Manager will give you an estimate how many people your advertisement will reach before you actually publish the ad. This is especially useful if you or your client are unsure about your budget or audience.

Once your ad campaign has been published, you will receive performance updates throughout the campaign. These results are available on the "Insights" tab in the Ads Manager. It is very important to take these updates into consideration throughout the campaign, as adjustments to the campaign parameters may be necessary to hit your performance goals - like increasing your budget, or reducing or expanding your audience.

If, for some reason, your ad campaign is completely unsuccessful, and Facebook Ads Manager is unable to obtain the results that were quoted to you when the ad was published - whether the issue is related to your budget or your ad strategy - Facebook Ads Manager will stop delivering the ad and you will not be charged if you did not receive results. This "guarantee" is especially important for first-time advertisers and small business owners that have a tight advertising budget.

Once your budget has been set, the Facebook Ads Manager will spread your Lifetime Budget out over the entire length of your ad campaign. Doing so may cause your Daily Budget to decrease, but Facebook Ads Manager will never exceed the Daily Budget you originally set. This ensures you that Facebook Ads Manager never goes "over-budget" on any aspect of your campaign and that you never spend more money than you are willing to spend on an ad campaign.

Tip: Set a cap on your expenditures, track how much money you have spent using Facebook's spend meters, and measure your campaign's performance using the ads reporting tab in the Facebook Ads Manager.

Tip: Avoid changing your budget type mid-campaign. Doing so will reset your budget, and this may alter the ad analysis provided by Facebook Ads manager. Also, you can use the Audience Insight feature in Ads Manager to help with your target selection.

Step three

The third step is to bid for your various objectives. For example, let us say that your chosen objective was to direct traffic to your website. In that case, Facebook Ads Manager will charge you when your ad is delivered to an audience that is most likely to click the provided link, which will then direct them to your website. You will not be charged when the link is clicked, but you will be charged each time the ad is shown to someone who has a proven history of following the links provided in advertisements. This is important because it prevents you from being charged if the same person clicks on your link repeatedly, which can happen by mistake or as a result of a malicious intent to abuse and misuse your ad campaign.

At this stage, you will also choose where you would like your ad to be placed on the Facebook platform. Ads may be displayed in the desktop News Feed, the mobile News Feed, or in the column to the right (outside of the News Feed). Displaying your ad in the column to right could be beneficial, as those ads are typically stationary and do not scroll away as the user scrolls up and down through their News Feed. Advertising in that right-hand column can generate more attention, or more consistent attention, from Facebook users. On the other hand - displaying your ad here may not provide greater attention, as many Facebook users rarely let their eyes divert away from their actual News Feed. There is no guarantee, so you may want to try a different ad campaign in each location, just to see what will work best for your ad sets and your business.

When choosing your ad location, take your demographics and target audience into serious consideration.

For example - should an ad be shown in the desktop News Feed or the mobile News Feed if the target audience is between 18 and 24 years of age? It should probably appear in the mobile News Feed, as this age group is much more likely to access Facebook on their mobile phones than on an actual computer.

Or - should an ad be shown in the desktop News Feed or the mobile News Feed if the target audience is between 65 and 80 years of age? It should probably appear in the desktop News Feed, as this age group probably does not access Facebook on their mobile phones, and if they do, they may find it difficult to read or interact with your ad set on such a small screen.

Tip: *Choose multiple placement options to give your ads the best chance of engagement.*

Tip: *If you believe that one ad set is performing better than another, change just one of the ad settings, like: bidding, budget, placement, or targeting. Keep all other settings the same. This will reveal which setting is having the most impact, allowing you to learn more about the demographics connected to your business brand, what works, and what does not work.*

Step four

The fourth step is to create a variety of ads and see which of those ads work best for your goals. You can use a combination of text, links, images, and video, and you can use up to fifty different ads in any given ad set. If one ad, in particular, is performing poorly, you can easily turn that ad off without altering or stopping the rest of your ad campaign, and without upsetting your budget. Best of all - Facebook Ads Manager never charges you for stopping or altering your ad campaign.

Keep in mind that your ads need to be eye-catching, otherwise audience members will scroll right past them without ever looking at what you have to present.

- *Video Ads:* keep the video short and make sure any audio attached to the video is neither too loud nor too quiet. Studies show that most people will click away from any ad video that lasts longer than twenty seconds.
- *Image Ads:* keep the images small enough to display nicely on a cell phone screen, and try to include some text on or around the image. Without the text, many audience members may be unsure of what it is you are advertising or what your objective is.

Another important thing to keep in mind when designing your ads is copyright laws. Be extremely careful with the images and videos that you use. Take advantage of websites like Shutterstock.com, whether you can safely purchase images or videos that are relevant to your product, brand, or company. Or, better yet, take the photos or film the videos yourself!

If your ad includes an image or video that you found via a quick Google search, and you did not obtain the appropriate copyright release, the owner of that image or video could allege theft, could send a "Cease & Desist" letter that would require you to stop using the image or video, and could even sue you and collect some of the profits that you saw as a result of the ad campaign their image or video was used in. Copyright laws are surprisingly strict, and if there is a copyright dispute, it can be a very stressful and costly situation.

Similar to copyright laws are "intellectual property laws," which are what protect writers from plagiarism. Be careful with what you write in your ad copy. You will want to make sure the text is original. You can do this by using various plagiarism checkers that are free to use online, like www.edubirdie.com.

Photo Ads: Using images is an excellent way to promote your work, your business, and/or your brand. It has been proven that using images online is much more effective in getting the attention of your audience than text copy ads alone.

Facebook photo ads are simple and straightforward. With the right image and accompanying text copy, people are much more likely to notice your brand. Photos are also excellent for increasing your audience's awareness of your products and/or services. People are much more likely to buy a product if they can see it first.

Consider using photo ads for any new products that your business is promoting. Photo ads are also very easy to make. You can simply add a photo to a page post, giving that post an automatic little boost. Photo ads work great for both desktop and mobile devices. As always, make sure the images you are using are either free of copyright or that you own the copyright or copyright release to them.

Video Ads: Facebook understands that people want different kinds of videos in different situations. For instance, if someone is on their mobile device, they are probably on-the-go and would prefer to watch something short. Meanwhile, if a person is on a larger device (like a laptop) and sitting on the couch, then they are likely more willing to watching a longer video.

For shorter videos, you might want to consider using in-feed ads. Whether your goal is to reinforce your brand or promote a new product, in-feed ads capitalize on quick, short spurts of attention from your target audience to promote your business.

Create a captivating video which quickly tells your story, and people, while scrolling through their feed, will stop to hear what your company has to say. Using video ads is a great way to drive sales. Furthermore, by combining video ads with product images and carousels, you can stimulate the interest of your audience and potentially increase your sales.

You can also create video ads that appear "in-stream," meaning the ad is shown after the viewer has begun watching a video. In-stream video ads can be as long as fifteen seconds, but the shorter they are, the better. Research shows that 70% of in-stream ads are watched to completion, with the audio/sound on. This allows you to deliver a more dynamic message to your audience.

Another advantage to using video ads on Facebook is that it allows your company to reach people that you might not otherwise reach with more expensive television ads. Research shows that Facebook video ads reach 37% percent more people in the age group of 18 to 24. Facebook is also creating new ways of using video to engage your audience. With Facebook 360 your customers can interact with the video to explore a 3D or panoramic environment. This is particularly useful for businesses like Real Estate Agencies - instead of posting a picture of a house, they can create a 3D or panoramic video of the interior of the house. This is much more eye-catching and attention-getting than a simple picture!

Finally, using Facebook Creative Hub, you can create "mock-up" or tester video ads, and then test them in real time. This allows you to see how various types of video ads may affect your audience and allows you to view these video ads from the perspective of your audience. This is especially important if you are interested in running a video ad in the News Feed of mobile phones, as the Mobile-view can restrict what appears on the screen. As always, make sure the images you are using are either free of copyright or that you own the copyright or copyright release to them.

Messenger Ads: Messenger ads are ads that appear in Facebook Messenger, as opposed to the News Feed of your audience members. Research shows that 2 billion Facebook messages pass between people and businesses each month. Using Messenger in this way is an incredibly effective way to engage current customers and to attract a wealth of new customers.

The best way to use Facebook Messenger, and to capitalize on its worldwide reach, is to place your ads on the Facebook Messenger home screen. This way, ads are mixed in with your customer list of conversations and are therefore difficult to ignore.

Messenger ads work in the same way that other ads do across the Facebook platform. Ads appear where they are most likely to boost your campaign, at the lowest possible cost to you.

When your customers tap on the ads appearing on their home screen, they will automatically and immediately be sent to whichever destination you selected during the creation of the ad, such as your website, your app, the product page you created, or a dialogue with your company on Facebook Messenger.

Using Facebook Messenger to promote your business has three essential advantages:

- You can start new conversations by using Facebook Messenger ads, which allows you to open a direct dialogue between your business or brand and the potential new or repeat customer.
- You can stay on top of Facebook Messenger conversations with existing or return customers by utilizing Facebook Messengers high-level view of existing or open conversations.
- You can re-initiate old conversations with customers that you have not interacted with or touched base with after a certain period of time.'

Below are the steps to take to create messenger ads.

1. Click create ads.
2. Choose messages objective.
3. Click the ad type messenger and select Sponsored message.
4. Chose which Facebook page top run the ad through.
5. After clicking the sponsored message, you can then have a custom audience based on your Facebook fan page messenger activity.
6. On placement level select automatic placement.

7. Click turn on when the messenger placement notification displays.
8. Choose your budget and schedule.
9. Click continue.
10. Choose image and text or text only.
11. Under page and links chose the page you want.
12. Select call to action, i.e. Learn more, sign up now, or contact us.
13. Click review order to check for errors.
14. Place order.

Each one of these steps is super easy. There are a few tips that can be used to make these advertisements more profitable.

- Tip 1: Only one message can be delivered to each person, within one ad set. In order to have more than one, you need to click Create Multiple New Ad Sets.
- Tip 2: By clicking show advanced options you can add additional targeting options. However, your audience size must have 20 or more people.
- Tip 3: In your edit placements section, you are only going to be able to select sponsored messages.
- Tip 4: The majority of your sponsored messenger ads will deliver in 3-5 days. If you want them to be delivered within specific times, then schedule them out for a week.
- Tip 5: There is a minimum bid that you can use. It will load in the bid strategy section for ad creation flow. In the US they recommend a bid of $30 per 1000 impressions.
- Tip 6: Schedule the ads to Run all the time. Sponsored ads do not support Ad scheduling.
- Tip 7: Optimization is set by impressions, the rate for sponsored messages is $30 per 1000 impressions.

Carousel Ads: Carousel ads allow you to use multiple images within a single ad. Each image can have its own link, and you can also use videos. Carousel ads allow you to showcase multiple products, various aspects of a single product or service, current promotions, or even convey a story about your company or brand that unfolds across each carousel card.

This ad format is dynamic and can be used to reach any number of your company's marketing goals. Carousel ads have a number of advantages over other types. Carousel ads give marketers a lot more space to be creative and engaging within the ten carousel cards available. They are also highly-interactive, allowing you to link to multiple websites or product pages. Your audience can also swipe or click on your carousel cards to move the story along, or visit whatever page you have linked to the image or video in question. And finally, because you have ten cards to fill with video or imagery, you have the flexibility to tell your story or feature your products in new and creative ways.

Whether you are showcasing multiple products, highlighting the various features of a single product, telling a story, or explaining a process, Carousel ads are a flexible and dynamic way to promote your business or brand.

Slideshow Ads: A Slideshow ad is like a video ad. It uses images, motion, text, and sound - all to tell a compelling or dynamic story. Slideshow ads work on any device and typically are not limited by slow internet or data speeds, the way some video ads are.

You can create a slideshow ad easily and quickly, whether for desktop or mobile devices, and you can use that slideshow to tell the story of your company, describe your product, or showcase a new line of products. You can use stock images made available by Facebook in the ad creation process, or even use existing video footage.

Slideshows are captivating, much like video ads are, but they are easier to create, less expensive to run, and less time consuming to maintain. They also tend to run more easily and more smoothly across all devices - from desktop to mobile, and everything in between. As always, make sure the images you are using are either free of copyright or that you own the copyright or copyright release to them.

Consider using a Slideshow Ad to determine what your audience may find compelling as a Video Ad. Slideshow Ads can be valuable "test runs" before you spend your time or money to create a Video Ad that may not generate the attention you had hoped for or planned on. Slideshow Ads are fast and easy to create and require very little planning on your part.

Collection Ads: Using a combination of video and imagery, Facebook Collection Ads are a great way to sell products, particularly via mobile phone. Because people are spending so much more time on their phones, and because this is changing the way they search, learn, and buy, Collections Ads are an ideal way to adapt to these changing circumstances. Your customers expect fast-loading, engaging, smooth video mobile experiences, so once a customer has tapped your ad, they can learn more about the features of your products seamlessly.

This ad format is seamless, and almost guaranteed to generate new business. Many Collections Ads include a video at the top of the ad, with a slideshow of images beneath the video - all of which are clickable and can provide your audience with direct access to your website, your product pages, and more. These ads are ideal for mobile devices because they tend to take up the entire screen of the mobile device - guaranteeing that the audience member viewing the ad is not distracted by any other content within their Facebook feed. You have their complete and undivided attention until they scroll away from the ad. As always, make sure the images you are using are either free of copyright or that you own the copyright or copyright release to them.

To make sure your Collections Ad is full of strong, effective content, consider trying the different aspect of the ad individually first. Post a Slideshow Ad with the images and test how well your audience responds to that Slideshow before including it in your Collections Ad. Furthermore, run a Video Ad alone as a test, before including it in your Collection Ad. This will guarantee that your Collections Ad is as effective as possible and that it will generate the response you have been looking for.

Step five

Once your ad set has been published, it is very important to pay attention to ad performance. Some ads may perform better than others, and you will need to find out why one ad performs better than others, that way you can adjust your ad set (and future ad sets) accordingly.

Facebook Ads Manager allows you to turn a particular ad off if you need to. You can also cancel your ad campaign altogether. In addition, if the parameters you set for your campaign are not generating any results, Facebook Ads Manager may waive the expense of the campaign, or reimburse you if they have already collected payment.

The following list will help you to understand the significance of the various results you may find in the Facebook Ads Manager report generator.

- Brand Awareness: This provides an estimation as to the number of people who may remember your ads within a two day period. This result is significant if you have objectives such as Video Views, Engagement, Brand Awareness, and Post Engagement. The reason they chose to a two day period is simply that studies show that if you recall seeing an ad two days after you initially saw it, you are significantly more likely to recall the name of the product or business a week or even a month later.

- Reach vs. Impressions: Reach is the number of people who have seen your ad at least one time. Reach is different from Impressions in that Impressions include people who have seen your ad multiple times, whether because they seek it out repeatedly or because it appears in their News Feed repeatedly.

- Traffic: This provides the number of actions your ads have contributed to your mobile app, and therefore recorded as "app events." This also provides the number of clicks your ads have received on desktop and mobile devices, which allows you to track how many people have used your ad to access your website - or whatever other clickable content has been attached.

- Engagement: This provides the total number of actions your ads have stimulated. This includes Facebook page "Likes" from ad engagement, the number of people that marked themselves as "Interested" or "Going To" an event your company has organized and streaming reactions from live broadcasts. This information is vital when determining whether or not your ad campaign has been successful.

Keep in mind that Facebook Ads Manager only bills you once a month, and only bills you for what has been spent on your ad campaign. Therefore - if you set a lifetime budget of $500 for your ad campaign, but only $25 of that $500 is spent in the month of January, then Facebook Ads Manager will only collect the $25 spent in January. This type of pay-as-you-go billing is incredibly useful for small business and those with small advertising budgets. Billing can be set up on an auto-pay schedule, using any major card. The auto-pay schedule can be customized so that you can even choose the day of the month that your payment is automatically withdrawn from your bank account or charged to your selected credit card.

Tip: It is better to turn off an ad or ad set as opposed to completely deleting them. Deleting an ad or ad set is irreversible. Turning an ad or ad set off is like hitting that pause button. This way you can turn them back on later, if necessary, and after you have adjusted whatever parameter was preventing your ad from performing well. You can also turn the ad set off if you suddenly find that you need to make an emergency change to your advertising budget.

Chapter 6: Instagram 2019

Instagram currently has more than 400 million users to the site on a monthly basis with more than a fourth of these using the site every single day. With numbers like these, it was only a matter of time before advertisers started taking notice and now more money is being spent on marketing via Instagram than ever before. While getting in now isn't exactly getting in on the ground floor, if you want to make money online, this is still a very profitable and fairly open market. You aren't the only one with this idea, however, so what follows are a number of ways to set yourself apart when it comes to advertising on Instagram.

Set your focus: Regardless of what you want to do with your Instagram account in the long term, the first thing that you will need to focus on is building a following, the more followers the better. The higher the number of followers you can boast, the more likely it will be that advertisers will give you the time of day and the more money you can get from advertising. In general, before you can start monetizing your Instagram page you are going to want to be able to prove that you have at least 10,000 followers and a strong following of individuals who check in with your page on a regular basis without actually following you.

The best way to start building your followers is with the right type of details in your profile. Information about yourself and the type of content you typically post is a good place to start, but only that, the best Instagram influencers include far more. This means including relevant keywords along with commonly used hashtags as this will make it less likely that you are simply posting photos into the void. This means you are going to want to start by coming up with a niche of photos that you are interested in working with every day for a prolonged period of time. If you have a topic idea but can't see yourself sticking with it for six months or more then you are going to want to head back to the drawing board as Instagram success should be measured in the long term.

Keywords and hashtags: Once you have a potential niche in mind, the next thing that you will want to do is to scope out other Instagram pages in the same niche and look to see what keywords and hashtags they are using. Keep in mind which pages you visited as you will need them later as well. While you are going to want to use popular keywords and hashtags, you are not going to want to simply stuff every one of your photos with as many as you can think of. Careful curation is key to attracting niche followers while not showing up so often that potential followers consider you spam.

Post, post, post: Once you have the limits of your content set, the next thing you are going to want to do is to post multiple times per day, every day. You will want to get on a schedule of posting and stick with it for long enough that people get used to checking back in with you at the same time each day. Once they are in the habit of checking in with you it is much more likely that they will follow you instead of having to track you down manually each time. It goes without saying that this will only work if you are taking high-quality pictures that people are actually interested in, if you aren't a photo-person then this online income stream probably isn't for you.

Take the right pictures: In order to determine the types of pictures that your future followers are interested in, head back to the pages you have already scouted out and determine which pictures are getting the most traction from followers. While copying pictures isn't going to get you anywhere, keeping these popular photos in mind when you take your own can give you some boundaries to your creativity that can be helpful to you in the long run. As you take pictures, focus on developing your own unique perspective as this is what followers are going to flock to your page to see.

Tag photos properly: Once you have pictures that you think potential followers will be interested in, it is important to go ahead and use the keywords and hashtags that you have come up with as often as possible. The more often various hashtags and keywords come up, the more likely your page will show up when those words are searched for. As your work expands, new keywords and hashtags are likely to become relevant, don't fight this and try and cram unrelated words where they don't belong, embrace the expansion as a way of gathering even more followers.

Join the community: When you are spending time on other influencer's pages, it is important to do more than luck, you are going to want to join the conversation. You are going to want to do more than simply like pages or include brief comments, the more you can prove you have something useful to say, the more likely that person's followers will check out your page as well. This means you are going to want to leave insightful feedback and start real conversations about topics that the niche is interested in. The more discussions you can start and participate in the better. These conversations shouldn't be thinly veiled adds for your own page either, focus on the quality of the content you are producing and people will track you down.

Tips for profile success

Choose the right handle: Your Instagram handle needs to be clear, simple, and easy to identify. You want to avoid using numbers or special characters in your profile handle because this will result in you being too challenging to find. The best handle you should use is just your business name, just like Nike (@nike), Walmart (@walmart), YumBakery (@yumbakery), TasteMade (@tastemade), NoRootsBoots (@norootsboots), and Target (@target) have. Using your business name is simple, easy to identify, and really starts building up brand awareness around your business so that people are more likely to recognize you in the future.

If your brand name is your name, you can simply use your name. However, this may not be ideal if your name is long, difficult to spell, or used by someone else already. In this case, you may want to shorten it to your first and middle name only or nickname like Jenni Farley of Jersey Shore did (@jwoww). Alternatively, if it is relevant to your business you may be able to add a simple prefix or suffix like Amanda Frances, a popular self-help personality, has done with her account (@xoamandafrances). Other examples of self-titled Instagram accounts that perform well and support in growing brand recognition include the ones held by Kim Kardashian (@kimkardashian), Oprah (@oprah), Deepak Chopra (@deepakchopra), Jess C Lively (@jessclively), or Will Smith (@willsmith).

The only time in which a special character may be deemed acceptable is if you use a period, which some companies have used. However, this can become very confusing for your followers as they may find themselves going to the original profile that has no special characters, rather than finding yours. For that reason, you should completely avoid adding special characters, strange spelling, or other unique elements to your handle. The more simple it is, the better it will be as it will make it much easier for your followers to find you online.

Take care with your bio: The most valuable real estate of your profile is your bio. On Instagram, you get about 200 characters, which can run out pretty quickly, meaning that you really need to spend time crafting the perfect one. Every word counts, and your bio should reflect exactly who you are as a company.

It really doesn't take that long of a time for you to go through and properly optimize the profile that you are using on Instagram, but it can definitely make a big difference on how many people will actually click on your site. It can also make a difference in how they view your brand. Some of the tips that you can follow to help optimize your profile include:

- In your bio, you should try to include the following information:
- Who you are
- What services you should provide
- Why should you follow them
- A link to your website for more information. You could even consider setting up a landing page that is specific for your visitors from Instagram, or you can make changes to the link to help promote a current campaign or other content.
- Make sure that the description and the images on your profile go well with the vibe that you want to see in your company.

- Use the logo for the company somewhere in the profile. This lets your users know that this profile is the official one for your company.
- Consider adding at least one brand specific hash tag to your profile. This makes it easier for your customers to know the profile belongs to you.
- If you are a local business or have your own store, consider including your physical location into the profile as well.
- Make sure that if you have other social media profile that your images, and any other content, stay consistent throughout.

Posting tips

Post at the right time: On Instagram, your audience will have a tendency to hangout on the platform at different times throughout the day, and throughout the week. Learning how to track your best posting times and post within these peak hours will ensure that your photographs get maximum engagement so that you can begin growing your account rapidly. With Instagram, the algorithm favors posts that are being interacted with quickly and genuinely, so the more likes and comments that you can accumulate early on, the better.

You can track the right posting times for yourself and your audience through Instagram's business analytics or through third party applications like PLANN or Iconosquare which both have intelligent and highly accurate schedules for you to plan your posts with. These platforms track your engagement and let you know when your profile tends to get the most views, likes, and comments through your new posts. Although third party apps will cost money to gain access to this information, it can help you rapidly grow your platform through having access to the right information to help you do so.

Post the right content: The trend on Instagram used to be to load your page up with selfies and have people liking your images, and while this behavior is still perfectly okay for simple sharing accounts, they are not ideal for brands or businesses who are looking to grow their platform in 2019. While selfies can (and should) be used to grow your page, you should refrain from having every post, or even every other post featuring you in a selfie. Instead, use selfies sparingly and place an emphasis on uploading other photos of interest to help you increase your reach in 2019.

If you do love sharing selfies and they do in some way relate to your brand, consider using your selfies more consistently in your story feed and less frequently in your actual newsfeed. This way, you can still share on-brand selfie images that can help you increase traction, but they do not dominate your feed and make you appear unprofessional or juvenile on the platform. These days, people prefer to see more thoughtful images that look similar to those that would be taken by professional photographers.

Be consistent: Having a consistent editing style will help you create some cohesivity in your feed. This makes sure that colors that are present in your photos generally look the same in every photo. Using apps like VSCO allows you to create presets so that you can use to utilize the same filter, temperature setting, contrast, highlights, etc. in every photo. This can be helpful, but it may be better to stick to editing each photo on an individual basis. This allows you to tweak different small aspects that benefit that specific photo. You can also use the filters in the Instagram app.

Photos with one of a few specific filters tend to get higher engagement than others, so using these may increase the favorability of your posts. Clarendon, Gingham, and Juno are the 3 most popular filters, followed by Lark and Mayfair. Using these filters, or similar filters from other apps, can increase engagement on your photos. You can also incorporate a specific personal touch that you add to each of your photos. Some people like to post photos with an element of darkness or shadows.

Doing this consistently can draw an audience that looks forward to seeing how you incorporate this element. It can narrow down the photos you are able to post, but it will help grow your following. Having one color that is present in each photo (for instance, a red shirt in one photo, a red building awning in the background of another, and a red coffee mug on a table in yet another) can be enough of an element of consistency.

Have the right captions: How you caption your photos can also be important. The caption should be relevant to the photo in some way, and it should add to the feel of the photo, not take away from it. Really long captions are a bit iffy in how they can read to your audience. An unnecessarily long-winded caption can detract from the beauty of your photo, and can cause your followers to not hit the like button because they get distracted reading the caption and scroll on.

A long caption that educates your followers on a topic within your brand can be a positive addition to your posts as it gives your followers something useful. This creates a value exchange.

Utilizing Instagram stories: Instagram stories are a powerful tool that can be used to not only nurture your existing following but also attract new followers into your business. When you use your Instagram stories correctly, you can create a significant influx of engagement from your followers, add a personal opportunity to connect with your brand and create a more interactive page overall.

On Instagram, people love interacting with the brands that they love and consuming as much of their content as they can, and Instagram offers plenty of ways for followers to do just that. As you upload to stories throughout the day, you create the opportunity for your followers to feel like you are genuinely thinking about them throughout the day, which establishes a connection of care and compassion between you and your followers. Not only will this help you maintain your existing followers, but it will also help new or potential followers see how interactive and intimate you are with your following, which leads to them wanting to be a part of your following as well!

The reason why stories works is simple, people are nosy and they like to know insider's information. This is not a bad thing, either, but rather just a simple human experience where we all desire to be a part of something bigger than ourselves and we want to connect with those around us to become a part of that "something bigger." You can position yourself as the facilitator of that "something bigger" by turning your brand into an experience that people can enjoy, and an entity that they can share an intimate and compassionate relationship with.

Stories give you a great option to do that because every picture or short clip you share reflects a part of your personal behind-the-scenes experiences. You can also curate your story feed to offer an even more exclusive and intimate feel by purposefully sharing things that will allow others to feel like they are genuinely connected with you through your feed.

Maximizing hashtags

Hashtags. You see them on practically every image that is uploaded on Instagram. Why do hashtags matter in these images and videos that get uploaded to the newsfeed? Because with a staggering number of images that get posted online daily by the millions of users around the world, delivering the right type of content to the right kind of people is difficult. Enter hashtags, the key to helping your content get viewed by the users who will be the ones keen on seeing it the most.

Want to maximize the potential of your posts being discovered across Instagram? Here are a couple of strategies to keep up your sleeve:

Use your hashtags strategically: Before every post is sent out, ask yourself how many hashtags do you think would be best? And which of these hashtags is going to benefit your ad the most? Having a quick think about these questions will save you a lot of time and prevent you from blindly hashtagging every word which you may *think* is going to help your post. Go with popular hashtags, but not the ones which are *too popular* where you run the risk of being lost in the tsunami of other content. 65,000 Instagram posts were analyzed by TrackMaven, and it was discovered that if you want your post to receive the highest possible engagement rate, then having 9 hashtags was the way to go.

Researching your hashtags: A simple, yet effective method is to simply do a quick search by typing in a few keywords on Instagram's search function. Then make a note of all the hashtags which get auto generated. It is also a great way to check up on the kind of hashtags your competitors are using. What sort of hashtags are your competitors or followers using at the moment? What are your influencers using?

Organizing your hashtags: Keeping your hashtags in an organized system is the best way to keep track of which ones you're using, how often you're using them and which ones have proven to get the highest number of engagement and traffic. You could either keep track of them using your own organizing system, keep them on an Excel sheet, or simply use Instagram's analytics tool to help you out.

Use the right hashtags
#Hashtags for Fitness in 2019:

- #fitinspiration
- #trainharder
- #fitfluential
- #running
- #yoga
- #fitness
- #winning
- #fitnessgoals
- #healthy
- #dedication
- #gymspiration
- #sports
- #gym
- #instarunners
- #workout
- #fitnesstips
- #fitfam

- #loveit
- #fitstagram
- #health
- #strong
- #training

#Hashtags for Fashion in 2019

- #modeling
- #fashionshow
- #instashoes
- #instahair
- #fashionista
- #trendy
- #luxurylife
- #cute
- #fashionable
- #instamakeup
- #fashionweek2019
- #photooftheday
- #model
- #instafashion
- #outfitoftheday
- #look
- #london
- #style
- #fashionblogger
- #fashiondesigner
- #fashionweek
- #design
- #instagood

#Hashtags for Food in 2019

- #instafood
- #yum
- #delicious
- #healthymeals
- #foodporn
- #nomnomnom
- #foodgasm
- #food
- #brunch
- #yummy
- #recipes
- #healthyeating
- #cooking
- #lunch
- #foodphotography
- #newrecipe
- #cookbook2019
- #healthyfood
- #breakfast
- #chef
- #healthycooking
- #wineanddine
- #healthy
- #diningout

#Hashtags for Travel in 2019

- #workfromanywhere
- #travel
- #summer2019
- #goexplore

- #digitalnomad
- #vacation2019
- #vacationtime
- #wanderlust
- #adventure
- #locationindependent
- #hiking
- #explore2019
- #travelpreneur
- #travelmore
- #adventuretime
- #roamtheplanet
- #workandtravel
- #travelblogger
- #travelblog
- #adventurelife
- #wonderfulplaces
- #traveller
- #doyoutravel
- #lovetotravel
- #adventureseeker

#Hashtags for Dog/pets in 2019

- #adorable
- #dog
- #cute
- #puppy
- #mypets
- #cutenessoverload
- #dogsofinstagram
- #puppylove

- #puppiesofinstagram
- #doglover
- #instapuppies
- #newpuppy2019
- #adventuredog
- #hikingwithdogs
- #dogsarethebest
- #puppylife
- #dogsarefamily
- #petstagram
- #puppypalace
- #lifewithdogs
- #pet
- #dogtraining
- #inspiredbypets
- #bestdog
- #weeklyfluff
- #instadog

These may be specific to the niche that they fall under but there are also ones that are generalized hot #hashtags that need to be considered for your Instagram profile. These are projected to catapult your engagement and Instagram audience to the top. #Hashtags for Instagram in 2019

- #fashionweek2019
- #newyear2019
- #newyears2019
- #musician
- #birthday
- #wedding
- #instalove
- #instafollow

- #followme
- #fun
- #happy
- #bestoftheday
- #workout
- #instagramhub
- #beautiful
- #smile
- #2019
- #aladdin2019
- #IT
- #cleaneating
- #red
- #love
- #tbt
- #iphonesia
- #igers
- #igdaily
- #blackandwhite,
- #stories
- #tweetgram
- #fitness
- #fit
- #instacool
- #musically
- #joker2019
- #instasize
- #photooftheday
- #nofilter
- #adventure
- #webstagram
- #picoftheday
- #repost

- #foodie
- #ootd (Outfit of the Day)
- #my
- #followback
- #likeforlike
- #instastyle
- #instamood
- #instalike
- #instagood
- #digitalnomad
- #travel2019
- #life
- #funny
- #travel

Now that you have your own cheat sheet for Instagram #hashtags it is time to start utilizing these to your advantage in 2019. Since a post on Instagram that contains a #hashtag get on average a 12.6% increase in engagement, it is a no brainer that you should use them in all your posts. #Hashtags help you reach a wider range of people that fall into that niche and will be interested in seeing your posts and reading what you have to say.

- #motivation
- #love
- #tbt
- #instagood
- #cute
- #Food
- #instamood
- #photooftheday
- #me
- #iphonesia

Try out a contest: Another thing that you may want to try out is running a contest. If you have a product that you can give away or something that you are willing to give away to help grow your business, then it may be a good idea for you to run a contest. There has to be a catch though. For example, for someone to have a chance of winning the contest, users need to repost a specific image and then tag you in the caption. Or you can invite your followers to use a special hashtag that you design and then use it on their own images.

If you feel like really expanding this out and getting other Instagram names on board, you can consider doing a giveaway. You can get on board with a few other profiles and influencers, and then everyone can be a part of this. This helps to give each profile or business a chance to reach new customers and can be a great way to build up your business like never before.

Instagram marketing mistakes to avoid

Don't be overly promotional: If your feed is filled with promotional content, your followers will receive more of a spam atmosphere from your blog. If your followers feel that they are disconnected from your blog, they may stop working with your posts. Some of your followers will eventually unfold. Make a balance between promoting your blog and engaging your followers actively.

Don't ignore the response/feedback you receive from your followers: You should actively seek your followers ' feedback. You can send them a questionnaire or talk to them to see what they really think about your blog. The response you receive from them could help you to work in areas in which you do not perform well in and can work to capitalize on areas in which you do well in.

Do not neglect captions: Try to prevent uploading images without subtitles. Subtitles help your followers gain more insight into the uploaded image. Captions are also what you use to communicate with your followers. The right types of headings give your followers the context of your posts and they can also contribute to your audience's response. Try not to go too far. 200 characters should be sufficient enough to pass on a message. Use emoji's as well, they can catch the eye of the viewer.

Don't neglect your community: Some people tend to think that their Instagram is just one way. They ignore the comments and messages of their followers. This never plays well. Your followers will feel that you are not interested in what they have to say, and they will flee. They may not even pay attention to your blog at all. Never wait for your followers to reach you, perhaps try reaching out to them!

Try not to underutilize the application: Use the Instagram stories, hashtags and inboxes to communicate with your followers and colleagues. Don't just take pictures, try attaching a link to your profile and explore the features. Instagram recently introduced a feature that allows you to upload multiple photos as a single post, try to make use of that. The more features you use; the more content you create.

Chapter 7: Paid Instagram Marketing

Paid advertising on Instagram is done the same way as it is on Facebook which means a majority of the information in chapter 5 is relevant here as well. In fact, if you start with Facebook before moving on to Instagram then all of your relevant choices will carry over. Overall, there are five different ways to create paid campaigns on Instagram including:

- You can create an ad in the Instagram app
- Through Facebook Ads Manager
- Using Facebook Power Editor
- Using Facebook's Marketing API
- Using Instagram Partners

Setting Up the Ad Placement

When you reach the stage of the set up for your ad campaign, there are quite a few options to choose from:

- The Facebook News Feeds – desktop and mobile
- The Facebook Right-Hand Column advertising
- Instagram
- In-Stream Video
- Instant Articles
- The Audience Network

For your first ad placement, you'll choose Instagram to get a new campaign on Instagram. However, you can choose numerous ad placements and use Instagram as one of the several options. It's possible to link several ad placements on Facebook allowing for your ads to appear in several newsfeeds and apps.

Ad specifications

There is more than one ad type to use when advertising on Instagram and the option is yours to choose which one best suits the ad you want to develop and post. Currently, there are a variety of different types of ads that can be used to market your ad, each one that would be perfect for a somewhat different marketing campaign. However, Facebook has more ad types than Instagram. It is extremely important to be aware of the different ad designs, so you'll be able to be knowledgeable in using them. Getting the highest ROI from Instagram marketing is what you want to strive for.

The questions that you'll want to be answered are:

- What are the different ad types on Instagram?

- What do you need to know to set up each individual ad type?

- What are the different ad specs on Instagram?

- What are the correct sizes for ads on Instagram?

- What examples of ads are the best to use on Instagram?

- Using specific types of ads – When should you use them and how to use them

Instagram gives you four different types of formats to choose from - carousel ads, single ad images, stories ads and video ads. The single image ads are the most straightforward, simple type of ads there is. Straight to the point, clear, concise, and they work brilliantly for ads which only want to feature single products or something with high visual appeal. You can't go wrong with this ad option.

Carousel ads are also known as multiple ad images. If you're planning to showcase several different products, it gives you more space to elaborate your content and the point that you're trying to make with your audience. Videos can also be slipped into your carousel ad selection to "spice things up" a little and create even more engaging content.

Video ads on Instagram work similar to Facebook, whereby they run on auto-play. They also start automatically playing without sound, although this is easily fixed by adding closed captions into your videos. The best video ads are kept at 60 seconds or less, and a minimum of 15 seconds at least to start.

Boosting your Instagram posts

Instagram's Ad system can be intimidating, especially when you're just started out and trying to figure out how things work. If you're looking to promote one of your posts quickly while still not entirely sure you're confident enough in your Instagram ad abilities, there's one option you could use to save the day - Boost Posts. With this option, you will only be paying to promote one specific post (so make it your best one!). As long as you have an established business profile on the social media platform, you can boost any post you have on your Instagram.

In your Instagram business profile, simply by clicking on a selected post, you will be able to see the option "Promote", which should be placed directly below the image. Clicking on this option will prompt you to select your focus objective, and you will only have two options to choose from. The first option could be to increase your website and profile visits, and the second option is to reach your target audience based on their location.

Influencer branding

One of the practices you can use for getting your brand out there and getting located is through using influencer marketing campaigns. Influencer marketing essentially means that you want to put your products into the hands of influencers and have them marketing your content, too. By having influencers sharing your products and brand with their own followers, you gain the opportunity to have your name put directly in front of their audience, too. As long as you are selecting the right influencers, their audience and your audience should be overlapping, meaning that they will help you gain access to your target audience much faster. With an influencer's seal of approval, you are far more likely to increase the effectiveness of your Instagram strategies and earn sales through your profile.

Launching an influencer marketing campaign first requires you to locate influencers who are likely to have the same target audience as you. Then, you want to consider how many followers they have and how active their following is. Influencers with more than 5,000 followers and with at least a 4% engagement rate should be considered effective early on. As you grow, you will want to continue looking for larger influencers who will be able to offer your brand even more exposure.

Influencer campaigns are costly in that you do have to offer free or discounted products to the influencers in order for them to have something to test, review, and promote to their audience. You will need to allot a budget towards this campaign that will account for the profit loss you will endure by giving away products or offering heavy discounts. However, as long as you are choosing the right influencer, this should all come back to you through their promotional activities.

Once you find influencers who appear to reflect your brand values and image and who have a similar target audience as you do, all you need to do is approach them. Typically, a well-put message that explains your intention and invites them to join your influencing opportunity is plenty enough to inspire an influencer to take you up on your opportunity. From there, you simply have to decide how much you want to give them, what you will compensate them with for their time and services, and what incentive you will provide their followers with to encourage them to purchase.

Tips for success

Keep it organic: The most effective Instagram marketing strategies are those that don't feel like they are actively trying to sell anything. Instead, if you are subtle about your branding then you will find that it is far more effective in the long run. Just because you are spending money on your Instagram ads does not make it acceptable to use pictures that feature a large logo or subpar images.

Additionally, it is important to never let your text take up more than 20 percent of any ad. If you try and fudge this rule then not only will your ads look cramped, they will get rejected as this is a firm policy for both Instagram and Facebook. When creating an ad you can use the provided grid tool to determine if a specific photo aligns with the current policy. Rather than using a text overlay you will find much more success by sharing the photo by itself and including any text in the caption.

When it comes to making your ad look organic, you are going to want to stick with pictures that have natural lighting and authentic looking pictures that are high quality. When it comes to showing off your brand's personality, you will also want to do so with the content and look of the picture, not by sticking a huge logo on all of your images. You should work hard early on to find the right mix of branded elements in your pictures to ensure that people who see it will associate it with your brand, without beating them over the head with the purpose of the picture.

Additionally, it is important to keep in mind that if you have too many focal points in your image then it becomes difficult for the viewer to decide what to focus on. Instead, you are going to want to stick to a handful of focal points, including a single branded element, and avoid borders or complicated filters completely.

When it comes to image quality, it is important that you only post high-resolution pictures that are clean and detailed. You should also strive to use images that relate to your niche and things that your audience can apply to their real lives as doing so will immediately improve your clickthrough rating. It is also important to keep in mind that consumers tend to trust user generated content compared to brand created content practically two to one which means that determining a good way to include this type of content in your advertising is almost guaranteed to generate a positive response.

It is also important to avoid resting on your laurels when it comes to the types of ads you create as your audience is always interested in something new and they tire of advertising quicker than anything else. One good way to split the difference between starting from scratch every time and keeping things fresh is to consider telling a variety of stories around a central theme. This way you will have some general guidelines that will keep you from having to reinvent the wheel with each new ad, and viewers will continue to see new things on a regular basis.

Look for opportunities for sponsored posts or paid shout-outs: When it comes to spending money on Instagram, one of the best ROIs is to find well-known names in your niche and then reach out to them about paid shout-outs or sponsored posts. This strategy worked for *Foundr* magazine which was able to pick up 500,000 Instagram followers in its first six months, 10,000 of which were accrued in the first two weeks of operation thanks to proper use of this strategy.

While you should certainly be willing to go the pay to play route when you are reaching out to relevant individuals you will want to start by offering a share for share with larger accounts. This is where two users share the other's content on their Instagram. While this is theoretically useful, the people you should be reaching out to will be significantly more influential in the space, which is why you will need to be willing to pay when necessary. If this is the case, then you may not need to pay for a full share, you could instead get a simple shout out for less money which is often nearly as effective as it make's that influencer's followers curious to learn more about you.

To get started with this type of approach you can look for shout-out groups related to your niche which often contain other Instagram marketers who can point you in the right direction. Using this approach is how Foundr was able to use a variety of shout-outs that cost about $100 each, by asking that the influencers include a call to action regarding checking out the new content. The results also work on a larger scale, if you have the funds to pull it off. In fact, one study estimated that paying those with more than a million followers to keep content in their feed for approximately three hours generates $5 worth of exposure for every $1 spent.

When it comes to reaching out to specific influencers the best place to start is with their bio. If, when reading their bio, you find an email address, then the odds are high that they accept sponsored branding placements.

Don't underestimate email: While having a large Instagram following is sure to make spreading brand awareness easier than it would otherwise be, if you are looking to generate serious business results then you are going to want to work to get your followers subscribed to an email newsletter. This is more difficult on Instagram than with some other social media platforms as Instagram does not natively allow for any live links in comments or captions.

Where you can place links, however, is in your bio link. This link needs to be short, memorable, and simple. Luckily, creating this type of URL is easy with bit.ly or other, similar, sites that allow you to generate a short, fully custom, URL. Back to the previous example of *Foundr*, using this method they were able to generate 30,000 subscribers in their first month. For a reasonable fee, companies like MailChimp will automate a majority of the email newsletter process so that you can turn your Instagram into a true conversion machine.

Take better pictures: When it comes to finding the right pictures to use, the first thing you are going to want to avoid is using a picture that you don't own. With so many different photos floating around online, it can be easy to think that a given picture is in the public domain, this is rarely the case, however, so if you are unsure of where a specific picture came from, don't use it. There are few things that can do more harm to your online persona than being accused of thievery, do yourself a favor and ensure your pictures are coming from legitimate sources. Additionally, it is important to avoid stock photo sites as much as possible because if users see the same picture in multiple places then they are going to naturally assume the content is the same as well which means they are less likely to finish reading whatever you have created because the impression is that they have read it before.

When at all possible, you are going to want to generate the pictures that you use yourself. Not only will this encourage your readers to feel more engaged with you over time, but it will also help keep your content feeling fresh. Depending on the size of the pictures you plan to use, and the quality of your smartphone, you may not even need specialized equipment. If you do decide to make your own photos ensure that they remain both relevant and visually interesting in their composition. A boring picture is still better than nothing at all, but only just.

Don't forget IGTV: The IGTV platform, which is built directly in to the Instagram platform, can be found on your home page. IGTV is designed to allow you to take videos with your phone and then share them on your channel for as long as you desire so that your audience has more to watch. IGTV is a great way to increase your following, as these videos stay in-place for as long as you leave them up, meaning that followers can look back through your IGTV channel and watch stuff that you put up days, weeks, months, or even years ago once it has been around long enough.

You can leverage IGTV to create new followers by creating excellent IGTV videos and then promoting them elsewhere online so that people are more likely to click over to your channel and watch. Once they see your video and the quality of the content you create, they can choose to follow your page in order to get more if they decide that they like you.

The big key opportunity with IGTV is that you can promote your IGTV channel just like you would a YouTube channel or any other free video content. By creating great content and then sharing it around you can encourage individuals to go over to your Instagram in order to be able to actually see the video. This means that you can funnel people from Facebook, Twitter, Snapchat, e-mail, and any other social media platform that you may be on to Instagram so that they can catch your free content and learn from it.

In order to make your content popular, you are going to need to make sure that the IGTV videos you make are worthy of receiving views. In other words, you need to be creating high quality, interesting, and relevant content that your audience actually wants to pay attention to so that when you share it to other platforms they are more likely to click through to your channel and actually watch the content that you created. The best way to create valuable content is to offer entertainment, insight, or guidance in relation to your industry so that your audience is more likely to pay attention to it and watch it.

Chapter 8: YouTube 2019

These days, building a YouTube channel really has to be done right if you are going to out-compete everyone else who is trying to create the same type of success that you are seeking. That being said, if you approach your channel with the right intention, attention, and desire to create success, you can absolutely out-compete anyone else who may also be trying to access your target audience. You simply need to have a greater desire, more consistency, and the right tools in place to help you access your audience in ways that actually work.

Creating the perfect YouTube page

Putting together a YouTube channel is pretty simple to do. The website does a great job of walking you through it, and with a little exploring, you'll be a master.

About section: The About section is often overlooked and not given nearly as much attention as it should in most YouTube profiles. This is mostly because when you look at somebody's profile, it's hidden in another tab, rather than right at front, in contrast to the majority of other social media networks where it's right at the front.

While your character limit is not nearly as cramped as others, it should still be short, sweet, and simple. Treat it like you only have 100 characters, and only put the most important things in there. Say what you do, your message, and your goals. You don't have to use hashtags.

At the end of your description, don't forget to add in all the links to your other social media pages, and if you have a website too. YouTube allows up to 5 links, which should be plenty. You can even customize hyperlinks up to 30 characters. You should also consider putting your business email, in case there are people who want to collaborate with you.

Your cover and profile image: Keep both your profile image and your cover image simple. Your logo can act as your profile picture, and for your cover image, consider a large image with your slogan, or a small description of who you are. Keeping it simple, at least at first, is a good bet. Just make sure it's visually pleasing.

Your YouTube trailer: YouTube actually allows you to choose a video to put right front and center on your page. One idea is to put together a trailer, clips and things all put together to really show what your channel is about. For just starting out, just keep putting your best work up there. The absolute best video you've got, the one that best represents your company and your channel should be the first video your potential customers see.

Creating quality video content

Starter tips: The following tips will help you create awesome YouTube videos:
camp

- Use a lot of light: you want your video bright, not dark, thus light is necessary.
- Use a clear background: filming on dirty and chaotic backgrounds (unless it's intentional) would have the video come out low-quality and make you seem unprofessional.
- Clear audio: audio quality is as important as video quality. Actually, most people have more patience for a poor-quality video than bad audio.

- Avoid shaky footage: it makes it seem like the person filming was ill or you had used an extremely outdated device. If you shake too much, use a tripod.
- Work on your camera presence: looking fidgety, nervous and uncomfortable will distract the viewers. You want to come across as someone who knows what they are doing.

Uploading your video: Uploading a video to YouTube is really easy. Open up the YouTube main page and along the top, you will see an upwards pointing arrow. Click on this arrow to go to the upload page, where you can select the video file that you previously edited. Once the video is uploading you can customize the headline, thumbnail, description, and tags.

Later on, if you want to make more changes to your video then click on your icon in the top left corner of the YouTube main page. A drop down menu will display, and you will want to click Creator Studio. This is where you can find all the tools you need to manage your YouTube page. In the right hand sidebar you can find your "video manager", here you can go to individual videos to edit their captions, edit the video itself, or change any other information regarding your video.

The importance of frequency: On YouTube, one of the most important things that you can do for your growth is to consistently publish new content for your viewers. Many people forget that YouTube is a social media website, which means it favors accounts that are engaging in regular sharing back and forth. The more frequently you upload to your channel and have friends and viewers engaging with your videos, the more YouTube is going to favor your content and drive you up in the rankings when it comes to people searching for your content.

Think about any other video-based system where episodes are frequently shared, such as cable, the more consistently content is released, the more people are going to tune in and pay attention to that content. The pilot episode may get a lot of hits, and then, after that, it may dwindle down, but the consistent releasing of new episodes keeps people coming back and watching more. Eventually, the audience grows again as people come back to learn more about the growing story line and are captivated by the show. The same goes for your YouTube channel: you might get a lot of hits early on, but if you do not maintain your frequency the content that you do share is going to stop getting views. You need to maintain your momentum and continue growing it if you are going to generate continued success with YouTube, which means that you need to ensure that you are consistently uploading videos.

Another massive benefit of frequently uploading new content is that you are driving new traffic to your channel on a consistent basis, which means that not only will your new videos get visibility but you will also increase the visibility of older ones. As people land on your videos, they will hopefully take the next step and visit your channel to see what other videos you offer. Through that process, if you have plenty of high quality videos uploaded that are relevant to your niche, these individuals will click through to your older videos and watch them as well. The more they do this, the higher your older videos will rank and the better your overall channel will rank as well, which means that your growth rate will increase exponentially.

Create a consistent intro and outro: An important factor that you need to consider when it comes to creating your YouTube channel is the consistency of your video content. You can create consistency by keeping your core message and approach the same, but you can further amplify that consistency by having short intro and outro clips that help introduce and summarize your videos. This is like the theme song and intro that your favorite shows play, followed by a short credits scene at the end of every episode, which helps you recall all of your favorite shows effortlessly.

Chances are you can still remember the *Friends* theme song, even if you never really got into the show, simply because it was used so many times and it played on television for so long. This consistency is exactly what you can create in your own videos by creating short intro and outro clips with music and information that introduces your audience members to your channel.

A simple intro is all you need, but it is highly recommended to keep you consistent and easy to be identified in the online space. Make sure that the music you use is royalty free, or that you purchase the rights to it so that you are not going to face any copyright infringements from your clips. Then, simply choose some high quality images or a short high quality intro film that you are going to lay the music over. Add in some words that introduce the title of your channel and the episode, and maybe your usernames for other social media platforms and your website, and you're done!

Try to keep your intro to under 25 seconds to ensure that you are getting the consistency across without overdoing it. If your clips are too long, your audience may click to a "similar" video for the same information because it took too long for you to get to the point, which would completely miss the point of this branding feature!

Post your content on multiple networks and advertise properly: If you look at some of the most profitable YouTube stars you will see that they link to their social media profiles in their description of each video. This is a method of cross posting for more added engagement. This also is a way of getting organic self -promotion. By cross posting your links you can gain more engagement and followers and build a wider audience that is loyal to your brand. Once your videos are uploaded share them with the other social media pages that you have. You can also cross promote between your different YouTube channels. With the advantage of YouTube's advertising options, you are able to promote your content on other channels that are relevant and relatable.

Monetize: Once your new videos are regularly generating at least 1,000 views per video you will know that you have enough of a subscriber base to begin to successfully monetize your page outside of just your affiliate links. Luckily, the key to doing so is already built into your channel through what is known as the monetization tab. This tab can be found in the options menu and it will let YouTube start placing relevant advertisements before your videos. You will also want to connect your channel to Google AdSense which, in turn, will turn on various advertisements based on each viewer's browser history. More information on AdSense can be found at Google.com/AdSense.

Both of these types of advertisements will start out with a pay per click structure, though if you reach enough subscribers you will eventually gain access to pay per view advertisements as well. If you plan on making money in this fashion it is important to never use copyrighted material in your videos. A pay per click structure typically pays out 20 cents per click, with 1,000 views being enough to assume 10 people will actually click on the advertisement in question. If you gain enough of a following to qualify for pay per view type ads, then you can expect to make roughly $3 for every 1,000 views the ad receives.

Become a YouTube Partner: While this final step is crucial when it comes to maximizing this potential affiliate marketing revenue stream, it isn't something you can do by yourself. Instead, all you can do is continue posting quality content, and when your videos hit a high enough number of regular viewers you will receive a letter from. Once this occurs you will then be able to place affiliate links directly in your videos as opposed to just in your video descriptions. This means you are going to want to ensure you shorten your links appropriately as no one is going to want to click on a URL that takes up three lines of the video description all by itself.

Tools for increasing reach

Tools, apps, and software to ease things and increase reach

Building a YouTube channel takes a lot of work especially if you are trying to grow your business. Fortunately, there are some amazing tools that you can use to help you with your channel. These tools and apps will help you to manage your channel, increase your reach, and edit your videos. Here are some of the tools and apps that you can use to enhance your YouTube channel.

- Tube Buddy: Tube Buddy is considered the single most useful YouTube toolkit. It is an essential toolkit that you need to have if you are to be successful. It comes with more than 60 different features that help you with almost anything that you need. Tube Buddy will generally help you to promote your channel and videos, ensure that you are productive, and also aid with your YouTube SEO.

- Snappa: If your YouTube channel is to grow and increase your reach, then you need a tool that lets you create excellent artwork and images. Snappa is among the top tools out there for YouTube videos. It will enhance your videos and enable you to come with great visuals through its premade templates. It is advisable to always use high quality image editing and enhancing tools for your YouTube and Snappa is excellent even when compared to other tools in the market.

- Creator Studio App: If you have a number of apps and wish to promote your business through them, then you will need some assistance. This is where the Creator Studio app comes in handy. This is a powerful tool that lets you do just about everything on your YouTube channel except perhaps creating the original video. You also get to find out how your video is performing and receive metrics and lots of other things as well.

- Wix: You will need this app if you plan to monetize your YouTube account. As a small business owner, your aim of using social media sites like YouTube is to help you find customers in order to sell your products for a profit. For this to happen successfully, you will need a website.

Affiliate marketing

You will also want to sign up for one or more affiliate marketing programs, most likely starting with what is known as Amazon Associates. Once you are a member of the program you can then link to any page on Amazon.com and receive a percentage of the total sales price of any items that visitors from your site purchase. The specific amount you receive per item sold varies based on the number of visitors your blog regularly sees. Don't be afraid to shop around when it comes to affiliate programs as they can vary drastically in terms of payout.

Once you start working as an affiliate marketer, it is important to not go overboard on the sales pitch as this is a good way to start losing all those viewers you worked so hard to gain. Instead, it is a better idea to create videos as usual but once a week introduce a new segment where you review a particular product that you think your niche would care about. This way, your viewers are getting useful content and you get to profit from the reputation you have created for yourself.

Depending on the goals of your content marketing strategy, reviewing products related to your niche or sub-niche is often one of the best ways to bring in new members of your target audience. A review of a product will naturally slip past the standard defenses that many people put up towards sales pitches while still containing virtually all of the same information of a good pitch without any of the traditional stigma that typically comes along with the process. Remember, a review can help customers avoid wasting their money on a shoddy product while a sales page is considered an especially pushy advertisement.

When it comes to these types of product reviews, it is important to be as honest about a product's strengths and weaknesses as possible. Especially when you first start affiliate marketing, if you take on a product that is questionable without pointing out all of its flaws and justifying your recommendation then you are likely going to train readers not to listen to you when it comes to products.

Remember your YouTube page is part of your brand which means you need to protect it first and foremost, no matter what the commission per sale might be. You want your reviews to include anecdotes of you using the product in question, with pictures. Your readers should be able to easily put themselves in your shoes.

The pay-per-sale commission model can lead to big windfalls for vloggers, but only for those who choose the right products to sell. As an affiliate marketer, all you can do is convince your readers to click the link in question, it is then up to the seller to complete the sale otherwise you don't get anything. As such, when it comes to products that you wish to advertise, be sure to check out the seller's page and ensure that it is going to hold up its end of the bargain.

The easiest way to go about doing product reviews is to focus on a single product or group of products with an exceptionally critical eye. This means you are going to want to single out the various weaknesses of the product or product line as well as focusing on its strengths and what makes it unique. It is important to keep in mind that this type of content needs to come off as unbiased as possible otherwise the illusion will be ruined. This means it is important to intersperse positive reviews with negative ones to allow your target audience to come to the right conclusions about your review integrity. When writing these reviews feel free to include two or three links where the reader can purchase the product if they are so inclined.

Broad strokes reviews: Depending on the type of products that are relevant to your target audience, you may find an in-depth review of products to not only be difficult to film but relatively useless as well. Instead, you may want to focus on brief reviews that typically include just a brief shot of the product and a few hundred words outlining the product's bullet points before including an overall rating and links to purchase if relevant. These types of reviews are typically most effective with cheaper products which viewers just want a little information on before making their purchasing decisions.

As an added bonus, these types of reviews often generate a higher rate of link click-throughs as users are more likely to click the link in question with the goal of finding out more information on the product. These posts are often going to include a round-up of likeminded products in each post and a ranking of the same from best to worst. This is because of the fact that your target audience is going to be much more likely to watch 1 video outlining 10 products than 10 videos outlining one product each as the single video will frequently be perceived as a more effective use of time.

Comparisons: If a product that you have a vested interest in stands up particularly well when compared to other products in the same category then a comparison piece can be a great way to make that superiority known. All you need to do then is to compare the strengths and weaknesses of each along with any feature parity and let the stronger product speak for itself. If you are particular fond of a given product but don't want to come off sounding biased than a comparison video is a great way to go about doing it. The more types of products you include on this type of review the better, if you do it properly you can attract plenty of additional traffic simply because you are a good resource for those looking to make the right purchasing decision right now.

Negative slant reviews: Negative slant reviews are different than outright negative reviews as the goal of a review with a negative slant is to convince those who are naturally contrarian by nature by including caveats in the review that are sure to hook them and draw them in. As such, to create this type of content you are going to want to focus on the positive qualities of the product in question before going on to lament how it is too complex, too expensive and the like which makes it a product that is only the most suited for the most committed or most experiences, users in a given niche. When done properly, plenty of people will be willing to prove you wrong and will put their money on the line to do so.

Chapter 9: Paid YouTube Marketing

Creating a campaign

Creating a paid YouTube marketing campaign is quite similar to the process you would go through via Facebook or Instagram. The steps are outlined below.

Creating your campaign

Step 1: Log in to your YouTube channel.
Step 2: On YouTube Ads, click on Get Started with AdWords for video.
Step 3: Select your time zone and currency of choice.
Step 4: Name your campaign.
Step 5: Sign in to your AdWords account.
Step 6: Login to your YouTube account again.
Step 7: Enter your daily budget.
Step 8: Click the select video button.
Step 9: Search for your YouTube channel.
Step 10: Select the video that you want to advertise.
Step 11: Write your ad copy.
Step 12: Choose your thumbnail
Step 13: Enter your landing page and click save.
Step 14: Create a new target group.
Step 15: Choose your maximum cost per view.
Step 16: Enter your keywords.
Step 17: If you'd like to target an audience further, click Add YouTube Search Keywords and Add Targets button to put more keywords.
Step 18: Save and start your campaign.

YouTube-specific ad formats

There are also a variety of YouTube-specific formats you can use for your ads, as well as some interactive elements you can add to give things that extra punch.

TrueView In-Stream: This ad immediately immerses viewers in your content. The ad plays for five seconds and after that, users are given the option to skip the ad, though it will continue to play if they don't actively choose to skip it. This type of format is ideal if you want to play an ad for your brand prior to, after or during related video content.

TrueView Discovery: This ad appears next to related YouTube videos, on YouTube search results, or on the YouTube desktop and mobile homepage. This type of advertising doesn't have an upfront cost, though you can still set how much you would ultimately like to spend. You pay for each click that you receive from a viewer whenever they click through and begin to watch your video. This option is great for reaching new viewers during the point of discovery when they are already looking to watch something new.

Bumper Ads: This ad is six seconds or shorter and plays before, during, or after another video, but unlike previous options, it is not possible for viewers to skip the ad prior to its completion. The rate for this is calculated per 1,000 views your ad will receive. This option is great if you are looking to simply get the word out about your brand to as wide of an audience as possible. The best ads that take advantage of this format are those that are memorable for a specific reason with a clear message.

Interactive options: You can add interactive elements to your video ads to drive deeper engagement allowing you to select the options that best support your campaign goals.

- Call to action overlay: This overlay appears once the video begins and is controlled by the viewer. They can close the overlay, or click on it and be directed to a website or YouTube channel that is predetermined.

- Card: This options plays a brief two-second teaser and is available in a variety of options. For example, you can link to a video or video playlist on YouTube.

- End screen: This screen shows up for a few seconds after your video plays and can be expanded to allow the viewer to uncover additional information when they interact with it.

- Companion banner: Accompanies a TrueView In-Stream ad as a clickable thumbnail. It can guide viewers to take an action such as "Watch more" or "Subscribe."

Watch the analytics

The first thing you want to monitor when you go to your YouTube analytics is your overall retained viewership ratings because this is what YouTube cares about the most. If this number is high, chances are the rest of your analytics are going to be higher as well.

If this number is low, or if it is dropping, chances are something in your overall strategy is failing and you need to start searching through the rest of your analytics to get to the bottom of it and see what is going on. Through this search, you can see where your strategies are falling flat and what you need to do in order to improve your content, your rankings, and your overall growth.

When you read your analytics, make sure that you not only pay attention to your overall channel growth but to your video performance as well. The performance of each individual video is going to tell you whether or not your strategies are working in each video, especially as your channel continues growing. As your channel grows and these numbers have a longer history, you can start recognizing the trends on your channel to get a distinctive idea as to what your viewers like and what they do not like on your channel.

These trends will show you everything from what titles draw the most attention to what styles of videos keep your viewers watching the longest, and even what content gets the most views in general. You want to start producing more of the content that meets these three criteria: gets the highest views, with the highest retention ratings, and the best engagement ratings.

So, videos that have many people clicking through to watch it, that have people watching it all the way through, and that have people liking or commenting on or subscribing to your channel are the videos that you want to favor. You can create videos similar to these ones, with new subject matter of course, and using or improving the strategies that you used on those videos to further increase your success on YouTube and get even more followers.

Tips for success

While there is no perfect formula for creating a successful video ad, there are a variety of things you can aim for to ensure your money is as well spent as possible.

Focus on the story of your brand: While bumper ads are effective for distilling a branded message down to its essence, longer ads are great for getting viewers invested in your brand's personal narrative. With that being said, the first five seconds are all you are typically going to have to capture the viewer's interest which means you need to start with a bang if you want anyone to come along for the ride. If you are going to include interactive elements then this will be the time for that as well.

It is important to leverage your best content in this instance as well, which is why you would do well to show various versions of your ad to a test audience for feedback before you settle on the one that best reflects your core goals and gets your message across as persuasively as possible. You will also want to ensure that it ends with a clear course of action that the viewer can take to move forward and actively consume more of your content. It is also important to ensure that viewers have time to act by including an end screen that lasts between five and 10 seconds.

Set reasonable goals: Many new social media marketers make the mistake of trying to cram as much into their first paid advertisement as possible in hopes of ensuring they get the most out of their initial investment. This is a flawed strategy, however, as by trying to do everything at once, they end up accomplishing far less than may otherwise be the case. Instead, it is important to pick a single goal per ad as this way you will be far more likely to actually accomplish it.

Chapter 10: Twitter 2019

Twitter has an incredibly high conversion rate for people who are on the platform promoting their brands. As you will learn about in this chapter, Twitter is far from going anywhere any time soon, despite what many people are eager to claim every year for the past few years. What's more, it can actually serve as a powerful branding platform for companies who share a similar demographic as the one that hangs out most on Twitter.

The approach that you have to each social media site that you work with should be a bit difference. You won't be able to use the same strategy that you do with Twitter as you do with your Facebook marketing plan. It is important that you learn more about the way Twitter works and the best way to use it in order to get the best benefits.

There are many different ways that a business is able to utilize Twitter in order to reach their needs. Some of the main ways include:

- Managing their reputation
- Branding themselves
- Networking so they can find other similar businesses and potential customers in the industry
- Interacting with their customers, and potential customers.
- Driving engagement for some of the promotional activities that they are working on
- Sharing the content and information that they have about their business and about their products.

Just like with all of the other social media options discussed in the previous chapters, most of these activities are going to have to do with interactions. It is not just about broadcasting out your content, like what can happen with Instagram and Facebook. Twitter works because of open communication.

Build a Twitter strategy

The first step in creating a strong strategy is having the right profile to back you up. Since Twitter is known for having an average of up to 80% of people who land on your page click your link, it is important that your profile gives people a reason to click through and check out your website. You can do this by ensuring that your profile looks attractive and features all of the information that people need to know about your business right off the bat.

When you first sign up for your Twitter account, you will be guided to choose a profile picture. Aside from that, you will need to click into the editor link to change your cover image, update your username, create your description, and add your link into your bio. You can do this by going to your account and tapping "edit."

The first thing you will want to do is change your username, as Twitter will have yours set to an automatically generated one that likely makes no sense to you or your brand. On Twitter, your username can only be 15 characters long, so if your brand name is longer you are going to need to find a way to shorten it without making it confusing or hard to remember or spell.

Next, you want to update your description to include a simple introduction to what your brand is about and what you offer. This should be engaging and interesting so that people can immediately resonate with you and your image and decide whether or not they want to follow you or click through to the link that you will also provide. You can provide the link on the same page as where you have updated the bio on your page.

Know your target market: You need to be very clear on who the target market for your business is. And which target markets you're trying to pull into your circle. If you don't know who your customer base is, you can't create the right kind of content for them to keep them coming back. Ask yourself who they are and how your business can help them. Ask what your business has to offer that would draw these customers in. Once you've answered those questions, then look at the content you are posting on your social media platform. Is it relevant, useful, beneficial, and interesting enough for your target customer base? Is this what they are after? Will this help them? Is the content relevant to your business? Does it engage the customers enough to provoke a response or reaction from them?

Be effective with your hashtags: Just like Instagram, hashtags play a key role on Twitter in helping to drive traffic and spot what the latest trending topics or discussions are. Hashtags are an excellent way for audiences to notice your posts. But there's one difference to using hashtags here compared to Instagram – on Twitter, keep the hashtags to one or two at best. Twitter is not the platform for multiple hashtags. Because the hashtag usage is limited, just like the content you're posting, you need to carefully consider which hashtags to use. Opt for the ones that work best with your business, and ones that are relevant. Don't just dump a hashtag in there for the sake of having a hashtag. It loses all value and meaning then.

Schedule tweets intelligently: Being active on Twitter does not mean infesting the timeline of your followers with 10,000 messages a day, or posting ten content within an hour and "sleeping" for the rest of the day.

If you want to attract - but above all, keep - new followers you have to intelligently measure your tweets and distribute them throughout the day. To facilitate this task you could use services like Buffer, which allows you to schedule the publication of new posts on Twitter and Facebook in a simple and fast way.

To subscribe to Buffer, connected to its homepage, click on the Sign in button and log in with your Twitter account. Then provide an email address and password to use to sign up for the service and create your first scheduled tweet. To do so, type the message to be posted on your account in the appropriate text field, presses the arrow next to the Add to queue button and select the Schedule post option from the menu that appears. Buffer is also available as an app for Android and iPhone, so you can program your tweets from the smartphone.

Taking the time to plan ahead of the holidays and any other special events that occur in your company can ensure that you have plenty of time. You can use this to pick out trending hash tags for your topics and create some high quality content without feeling rushed.

Instead of waiting until a few days before, you should make it your goal to come up with a campaign no later than two weeks before the scheduled time. There are also various calendars that you can find online that will help you look at the upcoming holidays so you can make a comprehensive plan of what you want to write your Tweet for.

Find the right people to follow: By following those that think exactly like you will help to increase your following and gain your brand a much better trust factor among your consumers. By following the ones that are gaining huge audiences you will be able to increase your reach through their re-follow. With Twitter, if you have followed someone and they like your content or re-follow you back there is an option to share the content that they like. This will spread the awareness of who you are and what your company is about. By following accounts that are not connected to famous people you will be able to get noticed for your follow and they, in turn, can share the favor and follow back.

Utilize the @mention often: On Twitter, there is an option for you to @mention others. This is a way to tag them in your posts. Anytime someone @mentions you, you should respond, however, do not only communicate with the ones that @mention you. You must communicate with others as well. It is best to find interesting topics that you are passionate about and then communicate with them about the topics that are hot topics. When you reply to topics that are hot topics you will be able to be seen by millions of other people that have been commenting on the post as well as those that will comment at a later date. This brings notice to your business.

You can also use the online target topics searching option to look for industry mentions and terms that would help you to find your subject matter. If you notice a Tweet that comes in which is relevant to your subject matter, then follow it and begin to communicate within the thread. You must be specific with the topics that you are looking for so that you can get a dedicated post that is about the topics which matter most to you. This will also allow you to interact with those potential consumers that genuinely care about your content.

Chapter 11: Paid Twitter Marketing

With millions and millions of tweets sent every single hour of every single day, it can be easy for the message of even brands that are well-known to get lost in the shuffle. If you are interested in using Twitter as a primary social media marketing platform then paying to make sure your ads get in front of the users who are most likely to actually use your product is a great way to ensure your message is heard above the cacophony that is Twitter at any given moment. Twitter ad engagements were up more than 50 percent in 2018 while costs were down making it a great time to look to Twitter to increase your social media marketing reach even further.

Twitter ad types

Promoted tweets: When you purchase a promoted tweet what you are essentially doing is paying to display a tweet to people who are not actively following you on Twitter. These tweets function just like any other and can be liked, tweeted, etc. Importantly, they also look like normal tweets with the exception that they have a small label that indicates they are promoted. Promoted tweets will be seen in individual user's timelines, at the top of relevant search results, and on user profiles and are visible on both the desktop and mobile version of Twitter.

Promoted accounts: Promoted accounts are a great way of reaching out to members of your niche who may not yet already be following you. Paying for a promoted account will allow your account to be seen in the timeline of potential followers, as well as in the suggestion field and at the top of search results. They are clearly identified as promoted, but they include a follow button as well.

Promoted trends: When a topic is trending on Twitter it is safe to assume that it is one of the most talked about topics online at the moment. Paying for a promoted trend makes it possible for you to move a specific hashtag to the top of the list. When a user clicks on your promotion they will then see a list of search results related to the topic, with your content at the top of the list. As more and more people get on board with the hashtag, your brand will gain additional exposure.

Twitter promote mode: While the rest of this chapter will outline how to set up a specific Twitter campaign, there is also an option for those who want to get started as quickly as possible. This mode costs a flat fee per month and, once activated, promotes the first 10 tweets you send out each day to your selected audience. With this option, you also get the benefits of a Promoted Account campaign.

The given estimate for the benefits from Twitter promote mode is an average additional 30,000 views as well as a net gain of at least 30 new followers per month.

Guide to advertising on Twitter

Getting started: First things first, if you haven't advertised with Twitter before then you will need to set up an account. To do so, all you need to do is to visit ads.Twitter.com and follow the provided instructions.

With that out of the way, you are now ready to choose an objective, in a fashion similar to the process as described in the

Facebook chapter. When it comes to specific options, you can choose from the following:

- Awareness: You want the maximum number of people to see your Promoted tweet. You're billed per 1,000 impressions.
- Tweet engagements: You want to maximize engagement with your Promoted tweets. You're billed per engagement for all engagement types.
- Followers: You want to build your Twitter audience. You're billed for each new follower, but not for other engagements.
- Website clicks or conversions: You want people to go to your website and take action. You're billed per click.
- Promoted video views: You want people to watch your videos or GIFs. You're billed for each video view.
- In-stream video views (pre-roll): You want to run a short video ad at the start of videos from Twitter's premium content partners. You're billed for each video view.

Moving forward: Next you will be taken the screen from which you can create your campaign, give it a name, etc. This is also where you will decide if you wish to start your campaign now or later. You will also set your budget on this screen, either what you wish to spend on the entire campaign, or what you wish to spend per day.

Next, you will need to deal with determining your ad groups, as well as bidding. Unless you are planning to heavily invest in your Twitter marketing you are likely going to want to choose just one group for now to maximize potential engagement. When you first start, however, you may want to consider playing around with timing, targeting different audiences, and the like, to ensure the option you ultimately go with best suits your needs. Should you choose automatic bidding, Twitter will automatically set your bid to get the best results at the lowest price based on your budget.

Select an audience: With the ad options out of the way, you will then choose your target audience in such a way that it serves to maximize your budget. You can target audiences based on language, location, age, and gender. You can target something as broad as a country or as specific as a single zip code. From there, you can get even more specific and determine what types of interests or behaviors you want your target audience to participate in. The Audience Features section will even give you the estimated changes to your audience size for each choice. You also have the option of uploading a predetermined list of individuals.

Launch your campaign: The last step is to review all of your choices and choose the option to Launch campaign to begin. Don't forget to watch your analytics after the fact to ensure you are using your money as effectively as possible.

Quick promote: In addition to the steps above, you can also use the quick promote option. This lets you determine your Twitter ad with just a few clicks. All you do is choose your preferred tweet and your desired audience and it is off to the races.

Conclusion

Thanks for making it through to the end of *Social Media Marketing 2019: How to Become an Influencer of Millions on Facebook, Twitter, Youtube & Instagram While Advertising & Building Your Personal Brand*, let's hope it was informative and able to provide you with all of the tools you need to achieve your goals. Just because you've finished this book doesn't mean there is nothing left to learn on the topic, and expanding your horizons is the only way to find the mastery you seek.

Now that you have made it to the end of this book, you hopefully have an understanding of how to get started building your brand, as well as a strategy or two, or three, that you are anxious to try for the first time. Before you go ahead and start giving it your all, however, it is important that you have realistic expectations as to the level of success you should expect in the near future. Having the wrong expectations this early in the process can lead to situations that feel like failures, even though they are really par for the course. This, in turn, can sour you on a potential marketing avenue, costing you who knows how much over what is essentially a misunderstanding.

Thus it is important to keep in mind that while it is perfectly true that some people experience serious success right out of the gate, it is an unfortunate fact of life that they are the exception rather than the rule. What this means is that you should expect to experience something of a learning curve, especially when you are first figuring out what works for you. This is perfectly normal, however, and if you persevere you will come out the other side better because of it. Instead of getting your hopes up to an unrealistic degree, you should think of your time spent building your brand as a marathon rather than a sprint which means that slow and steady will win the race every single time.

Finally, if you found this book useful in anyway, a review on Amazon is always appreciated!

Social Media Marketing 2019

The Power Of Instagram Marketing - How to Win Followers & Influence Millions Online Using Highly Effective Personal Branding & Digital Networking Strategies

Robert Miller

Table of Contents

Introduction

Congratulations on getting a copy of *Social Media Marketing 2019: The Power Of Instagram Marketing - How to Win Followers & Influence Millions Online Using Highly Effective Personal Branding & Digital Networking Strategies*. While it can be difficult to see a way to break through the noise of the millions of other Instagram marketers out there, once you do you will find a world of conversions just waiting to be yours for the taking.

In order for you to help unlock this world for yourself, the following chapters will discuss everything you need to know in order to start successfully using Instagram for your social media marketing needs. First, you will learn everything you need to know in order to get started on Instagram as quickly and effectively as possible. A big part of this is creating the right profile, which is why this important topic is outlined in great detail in this chapter.

With that out of the way, you will then learn all about the importance of choosing the right niche, as well as how to choose one that will be profitable in the long run. You will then learn how to create content that your niche will find interesting, as well as how to generate loyal followers who will ultimately be primed to learn more about whatever it is you are selling. This then leads to a discussion of converting your followers into paying customers, as well as what you might sell them once everything is up and running and how to go about creating a long-term sales funnel to ensure the conversions never stop rolling in. Finally, you will find solid social media principles to follow as well as social media myths to avoid.

There are plenty of books on this subject on the market, thanks again for choosing this one! Every effort was made to ensure it is full of as much useful information as possible, please enjoy!

Chapter 1: Getting Started on Instagram

An amazing 70 percent of Instagram posts will not be seen by more than a few dozen users. Why is this? Instagram operates the same way as all search engines (no matter how aesthetically pleasing in their presentation) based on an algorithm. The Instagram algorithm computes what content will be displayed to what user under what specific circumstances. It is the wise Instagrammer who observes, researches, and remains curious about the algorithm and what behaviors it "rewards" for posters, and which behaviors get "punished" by being left in the visual dust.

To be a successful influencer, you have to invest the time in yourself and in your craft. It is important to figure out the goals you want to achieve. Your success will not happen overnight because you put out one great piece of content. You need to be putting out great content daily. You have to make yourself relevant and your post must be relatable to your target audience. Tell a story through your post and make sure it will be taken seriously, is very effective, and potentially becomes a topic of conversation. The internet is bursting at the seams with information so if your content does not stand out and grab the attention of the consumer, it becomes noise which is ultimately blocked out. Instagram's user base is growing faster than any other social media platform, and current predictions show they will add an additional 100 million users in 2019 alone.

Influence is commonly mistaken with the audience, which is not the case. Markerly did a recent study on Instagram and after analyzing 800,000 users showed that "micro-influencer" (those with roughly 5,000 to 100,000 followers) influence outperformed that of mainstream celebrities. People are trusting peer recommendations more so than the brand itself, so a target audience needs to trust and value the influencer's opinion on a product or topic. Environics Communications published a survey earlier this year in which they asked people to rate their trust in sources of information regarding products, services, brands, or organizations. Not surprisingly, people came in at the number one spot through sampling, followed closely by word-of-mouth recommendations.

Features of Instagram: Instagram Questions – This feature was introduced in July 2018 and allows Instagram users to answer questions posted by their followers, although the answers to questions are not anonymous, you can post them to your story, and the name of the questioner is anonymous. This feature is very popular among users.

Instagram Direct – Direct allows you to share photos, videos, hashtag pages, profiles, and locations directly from your news feed with a single person or small group of people. You can access your inbox at the top right of the feed page from the inbox icon.

Instagram Stories – Stories allow users to post a picture/video selection in one story. This relatively new feature works much like Snapchat stories and after 24 hours, your story will disappear. They are not posted on the profile or news feed of the user. Instagram stories allow the same configuration of privacy as Instagram users. For example, if the user has a private account and posts a story, the story can only be viewed by user friends.

Instagram Statistics: On Instagram, 71 percent of 18-24-year-old individuals are using the platform to connect with friends, family members, and influencers and brands that they enjoy following. Of this sector, more than 35 percent of these individuals check the platform multiple times daily, and another 22 percent check it at least once per day. This means that, if you position yourself correctly, you have the capacity to reach up to 57 percent or more of your target audience through just one properly created, positioned, and scheduled post.

It's not just 18-24-year-old people spending time on Instagram, either. In fact, 30 percent of the users are aged between 25 and 34 years old, and another 17 percent are aged between 35-44 years old. There are more than 1 billion active monthly users on Instagram, which means that there is a massive opportunity to connect with the right people and start making serious waves in your business.

What's more, it is estimated that over a third of Instagram users have used the app to purchase products online. Thus, any marketer could tailor his brand and products to the Instagram audience and get a piece of the pie. Instagram users have been shown to be very responsive toward ads. The click-through rates are high and so is the engagement. As long as a marketer crafts a powerful brand message, they stand to gain an ROI from Instagram.

Aside from the statistics of which demographics are spending the most time on Instagram, it is also worth noting that all of these individuals are interested in a wide range of niches. That means that they are willing to follow almost any brand that interests them, regardless of what niche that brand is from. There are even dentists who are making a massive impact on Instagram, which is huge considering that many people are afraid of the dentist! By connecting with their audiences through this platform, businesses of all shapes and sizes are able to start creating positive connections with their audience which means that they are able to increase their brand recognition and their revenue simply by being on Instagram.

Every marketer understands the need to watch their performance, they want to know where their leads are coming from to ensure they can adjust their marketing strategies and boost lead generation. The Instagram ad platform enables marketers to see link clicks, leads, conversions, ad cost per result achieved. This can be very helpful in saving money. For instance, if you launch a campaign that attracts no results at all, it would be far easier to halt the campaign, do some major overhaul, before resuming the campaign. But the biggest advantage of this feature is that it lets marketers understand where their customers are stemming from. Thus, they can come up with more strategies to capture their target audience.

How do you use it? It is used daily to share photos and videos, watch Instagram TV, and stream live. You create an account and from there you can explore all the tools it offers, including a story that you can add to every day, tags that you can look up and even private messaging like Facebook. Once you create an account, the app shows you exactly how to navigate your Instagram account, which should allow you to use the app with little to no questions

More engagement from users: Depending on the quality of your content, some of the updates that you do on Twitter and Facebook will be ignored by the user. This isn't quite the same when it comes to users of Instagram. When you have an Instagram account that is active, and you fill it up with content that is interesting and valuable to your customer, you will be able to increase the engagement you have with your audience to crazy levels. In fact, a study that was just done by Forrester found that posting on Instagram could result in 58 times more engagement per each follower you have compared to Facebook, and 120 times more than you get on Twitter.

One of the reasons why brands find so much success with Instagram marketing is because of the nature of the content. It's photo-centric. People are more likely to remember what they saw as opposed to what they heard. Thus, marketers utilize this opportunity to create amazing content that captures their users' attention. With Instagram, photos and videos are enough, and you don't necessarily have to put text. And nowadays people are shifting from consuming text content into consuming more videos and images. Instagram has a leg up on other social media advertising platforms as well as traditional advertising platforms.

Whether you are a business trying to grow your reach or an individual who is looking for ways to earn money on Instagram, this engagement is key. It means that people are actually looking at the content that you post. It means they are liking it, commenting on it, and leaving you questions and advice. This makes it easier for you to sell products to them and can increase the amount of money that you can make on this site.

Building up your personality and trust with the customer: With branded content helping you to gain more engagement, one of the best things about working with Instagram is that it helps you to build up trust. Your customers are never going to purchase anything from you if they don't have trust in you, and without a good emotional connection, you are going to lose business to the competition.

With Instagram, you can build up this trust and this emotional connection, which can then help you to reach more customers overall. Instagram makes it easy for you to share the experiences that occur each day with your business, in a manner that is casual and informal, which can give a more personal feel to the business. This is something that a lot of your customers are going to like and can help you to grow by leaps and bounds.

Decide if it is the right choice: The last thing you need to consider when it comes to deciding whether Instagram is the right choice for you or not is to determine if it is going to be more effective in meeting your current objective over any other social media site out there. This does not mean that you cannot span your objective across multiple platforms. Most brands will do this. However, it does mean that you need to decide whether or not Instagram is the right investment of your time and funds right now.

If you feel that Instagram does have everything you need in order to expand effectively, then chances are Instagram is a great choice for you. Again, it is recommended that every brand be on Instagram and get to building their platform as soon as possible since Instagram offers so many valuable resources and benefits. However, if for some reason you do not feel that your own objectives will be met through Instagram, you might consider either adjusting your objectives to fit the platform's abilities. This way, you can still gain the benefits of being on Instagram in a way that meets your needs and the investment that you are willing to make into the platform itself.

Getting started on Instagram – an overview

Choose a niche: The first thing you are going to want to do is to determine what type of potential customers you are going to be marketing to. The best potential customers are those who are already into a hobby or interest that is relatively high end (to ensure discretionary income) as well as one that promotes the idea of regularly purchasing new stuff to support it through a never-ending cycle of new products. Something you are already familiar with is also ideal, otherwise, you will need to be prepared to do some research and learn the ins and outs of the niche you have chosen.

This means you are going to want to visit spots on the internet where your target audience hangs out. Learn what types of things are important to them and the types of products they seem to buy most frequently. Learn their thought processes and the slang they use, if you sound like you are one of them then they will naturally be more willing to accept your opinion when you tell them to buy one product over another.

Create social media goals: It is important to realize that social media works differently for different business models, so approaching your social media goals requires you to consider what exactly social media can do for you and how you can maintain your image while incorporating social media into your strategy. For example, if you are a lawyer you may not want to use social media as openly as an influencer would because you cannot be sharing that much information freely online without tarnishing your image or taking away from who you are.

In certain industries, you are going to need to be more conservative in your approach, which means that your goals should reflect these conservative social media values. So, if you were a lawyer on Instagram, rather than being open and sharing snippets of your life online, you would likely refrain from using stories or IGTV altogether and instead simply create posts on your feed. These posts should be targeted specifically toward your target audience by providing them with the information that they need to know that they need you in your corner, then direct them to your website or your phone number so that you can talk privately with them. In this scenario, your social media goals would be entirely to get people to contact you, rather than to build a massive following and become a well-liked influencer in your industry.

You can determine which style of social media goals you need quite simply: if you run a more professional business where you need to keep a large portion of information private, then you need to use social media to drive people to contact you. If you run a brick and mortar store, then you need to use social media to drive people into your store so that they can shop with you. If you run an online business, then you need to build your following so that you can market to a larger audience.

Create a bio: Do you have a solid bio? This is important and tells people who you are! It also lets them know what you do and what your personal brand is all about. You will want this to trickle over to your content so you remain consistent in your voice and your brand becomes recognizable. Include imagery that is appealing visually and include text that elicits emotion, creating a connection early on with your viewers.

Create an attractive feed: Creating an attractive feed is not too hard, as long as you know what it is that you are trying to create. If you are unsure, take a moment to scroll back through the pages of your competitors and see what they are doing. At this time, see what colors seem to be trendy and common, as well as what the themes tend to be with your audience. Although choosing your own color palette and theme is important, if you choose one that is too different from what the rest of your niche is using you may set yourself too far apart. In this case, your edge would become the ledge you leaped off of and your brand will become irrelevant.

When you are posting, there are four types of posts you need to know about: promotional, entertainment, quotes, and reposts. These types of posts are the only types you will be using, so knowing how they work, when to use them, and how to incorporate them in your feed is important.

Organizing everything: It is important that you know how to organize these posts in a way that appeals to your audience both visually and mentally. You want a feed that looks attractive, but you also do not want your audience to feel like you are hammering them with sales pitches all the time. Ideally, you should post approximately three times a day. During these three times, aim to post two non-sales posts and one sales post. This means you should be posting seven sales posts per week. Of those posts, make about two or three of them hard pitches and keep the rest of them as soft pitches. This means a couple will directly ask for the sale whereas the others will highlight the benefits of the product and encourage your audience to think about it or educate themselves further.

Determine engagement: In addition to followers, you need to review your engagement level. Having a massive following could be viewed as less powerful if your followers are disengaged. If no one interacts, the message becomes diluted and has no impact. Instagram has over 700 million monthly users, placing it well ahead of Twitter (more than double), Snapchat, and Pinterest, so it really shouldn't come as a surprise this is where influencers are migrating to. Instagram users not only actively seek content from their favorite brands or influencers; they want to consume it! Take advantage of the massive user base.

Get paid: At this point in the game, you should have a clear understanding of your personal brand, your market, and who your target audience is. Create a list of prospective sponsorship opportunities. Start with the marketing department or do a quick scan on the company website to see if they have employee profiles posted. It's a fact, businesses love numbers. If you can get them in front of 500,000 sets of eyeballs, tell them that! You should connect so well with the people they are wanting to target because you are their target! This is powerful and should certainly be used in negotiations. Do your homework and have a compelling story to create an emotional connection that sets you apart from other influencers and remember, it can be done!

Chapter 2: Build the Right Profile

When you first get started on Instagram, you may have a few followers. You may have some people who come from your email list, some followers from your other accounts, and some who just randomly find you when they are searching around the platform. But the truth is, your following in the beginning, is going to be pretty small. Many people may not even know you are there so if you want to extend your reach and get the most out of this platform, then you will need to start by perfecting your profile.

Choosing Your Handle: The Instagram handle that you choose needs to be clear and easy to remember, otherwise your audience may not be able to find you again once they leave your account. As well, you want to make sure that the moment people see your username they can make some form of clear connection between who you are and what your company does, otherwise they may not be tempted to click onto your profile page.

In general, most brands will simply use their company names for their handles, as this makes it easy for you to be found on Instagram. For example, Nike, Adidas, Walmart, and Nordstrom all use their brand names for their usernames on social media platforms, as this makes it straightforward for them to be located. If you are a personal brand, you may need to change the way you approach your social media to ensure that you are able to be located and recognized by those around the internet.

When you are making your username, refrain from using odd spellings, usernames that are similar to what has already been used online, or different characters or numbers in your username. Unless a character or number is a part of your brand name, attempting to make your username unique by adding these characters will instead just make it more challenging for you to be found. Remember, this is how people are going to look you up and this is the name that people are going to remember you by, if you want to have people easily able to recall you and locate you, you need to create both a username and a brand that people will remember.

Writing a bio that sells: On Instagram, you are offered a 150 character bio where you can give people an idea of who you are, what you stand for, and why they should be interested in your business. This bio is short, so you need to use your character count wisely so that you can say everything you need to say. You also need to make sure that you are keeping your bio catchy and interesting so that people are attracted to it and curious to learn more about when they find your profile.

When it comes to writing a bio that sells, there are a few different things you can consider that will help you really sell your profile and encourage people to follow you and check in frequently. The first thing you can try is listing your skills on your profile. This is especially helpful if you work alone, such as if you are an influencer, personal trainer, or fashion model. Saying something like "Recipes | Fitness Tips | Holistic Living | Plant Powered" is a great way to show what you are all about and make it simple for your followers to know exactly who you are and what you offer.

If you want to use more complete sentences, you can use a motto or a quote that is relevant to your audience. For example, Milk Makeup's bio says, "It's not just about how you create your look; it's what you do in it that matters. #liveyourlook" This type of bio shows your potential customers what matters to you, and quickly helps them determine whether your values are aligned or not.

Adding your email to your Instagram bio is always a good idea too, particularly if you are using a personal profile or if your business call to action is not based on emailing you. You can provide your email as a way for people to contact you, making it easy for potential customers, collaborators, or the press to get in touch with you to learn more.

Link: Instagram allows you to post a single link on your profile. Naturally, this should be a link to your website. However, if you do not have one you may prefer to post a link to your second most-used social sharing site. Alternatively, there are some companies that have developed platforms that allow you to post a single link on your Instagram page that will then take your followers to a landing page that allows them to choose what else they want to see from you. On this landing page, you can add other social sharing sites as well as your website. Companies that offer services like this include ones like LinkTree.

Point of contact: Once you convert your page to a business page, which can be done during set up or in the settings section of your completed profile, you are also given the opportunity to include a point of contact and the address of your business. Your point of contact should include your email, so be sure to create a new and more professional email for your business if you do not already have one. You can also add your phone number if there is one that your audience can reach you at. If you do not plan on having customers call you directly or you do not have a business number, you can skip adding your phone number. If you have a spot where your company is based out of, for example, a storefront, you can also include your address here so that your audience can find you locally if they choose to look.

Profile picture: Your profile picture needs to be something professional and identifiable. The best picture for a company to use in their profile picture is a logo of their company. This begins to build brand awareness and makes it so that when people scroll past your profile they remember exactly who you are. If you do not have a logo yet, you can consider getting one made by a freelancer on Fiverr, Upwork, or 99 designs. Fiverr and Upwork tend to run on the cheaper side of things, allowing you to get your logo for anywhere from $5-$10 while 99 designs are more expensive, but it does allow you the opportunity to get a wide range of designs to choose from and they tend to be higher quality.

Choose a profile theme: Themes are important for two main reasons. They are going to organize and focus your content, and they ensure that people know the general idea of the content they will see on your profile. It shows off your personality to the viewer so they know exactly what they are getting into on that page. These themes can also do wonders when it comes to streamlining your content creating process. This provides you with some boundaries to know what needs to appear on your page.

The benefits of Instagram business accounts: There are a handful of reasons as to why brands are choosing to use business accounts on Instagram, including many additional features that come in handy when you are running a business on the platform. Two of the biggest reasons why business accounts are preferred it's because they allow you to provide a location for your followers to see, as well as a call to action. If you are a local business, having your location displayed at the top of your profile can make it much easier for your potential clients to find you and begin visiting you in person. If you do not run a local business, such as if you have many locations, or if your business is entirely online you can always leave this information out to avoid confusing your followers. Having a call to action is also great because it offers a quick one-click feature for customers to get in touch with you so that they can learn more about your business.

Another major benefit to having your business account turned on is that your Instagram will begin tracking analytics on your page, posts, and link. Instagram's analytics will tell you about information such as how many followers you have grown by, what your most popular posting time is, what your most popular image is, and how many people are clicking through your links. They will also give you some information as to who your demographic is including what gender they are, what age range they fall under, and where they tend to be located. Having access to this type of information helps you determine whether your content is effectively reaching your targeted demographic or not.

Finally, Instagram's business accounts have the added benefit of being able to run promotions and ads on the platform. If you have a business that you want to be running ads for, this is the only way to gain access to this feature which makes it well worth it for you to make the change. Basic profiles do not have access to this feature, so you will not be able to run promotions on your basic account if you do not decide to take this step.

Changing over your personal account is easy, all you need to do is follow the steps outlined below, please note that you will need an associated business Facebook account to proceed:

How do I change my personal account to a business account?

- Go to your profile and tap the setting button
- Tap Switch to Business Profile
- Tap Switch to Business Profile and select the Facebook Page you'd like to associate with your Business Profile on Instagram with
- Make sure your profile is set to Public. Note: Private accounts can't switch to Business Accounts
- On the Set Up Your Business Profile page, review your business's contact information, make any changes and tap Done

Depending on how frequently you post, comment, like and engage with your audience, depends on how quickly your data is ready to view. Usually, you can see it over the next few days.

Improve your SEO

One of the first things that you are going to want to do when it comes to maximizing the impact of the content you are creating is to ensure that members of your target audience can find your content as easily as possible. The most effective way to do this is to ensure that your search engine optimization (SEO) is on point. The more effective your SEO is, the greater the possibility that your site will be ranked on the top page of popular search engines. This, in turn, will bring in more of your potential target audience without any extra effort on your part.

To improve the SEO of your page you are going to want to include common keywords that your target audience is likely to plug into a search engine if they are flying blind on what they are looking for in particular. If you still have the research from when you were looking for the right niche, then this will be a good place to start. Regardless, it is important to limit your keywords to 60 or fewer characters a piece. If you need help coming up with the right keywords, consider the following:

Consult your favorite search engine: For unsuspecting members of your target audience, the most likely way that they are going to stumble upon your content is through one of the major search engines which means that they are the best place to start when it comes to determining the best keywords to use for your site. In order to take advantage of this fact, all that you are going to have to do is to plug your niche or sub-niche into the search bar and see what results autofill from there. Be sure to keep an eye out for options that are suggested before you have finished typing completely as well as once you have finished the entire word or phrase. Additionally, you are going to want to scroll down to the bottom of the first page and look at related search results for more ideas that you may be able to use.

The results are going to be the major topics that people consider when they are searching for your niche and thus bear your consideration as well. While it's true that the more major search terms you can include in your keywords the better, it is important to not simply flood your page with keywords that don't have anything to do with the content you provide. The amount of time that users spend on a given page is also a factor in search engine ranking which means that lots of hits that only last a few seconds will do you more harm than good in the long run.

All told, you are going to want to come up with around five truly strong keywords that manage to sum up your page as a whole. You can then base your entire SEO strategy around them to ensure that you rank as highly as possible on those searches. The more specific you are, the greater the odds that you will end up on the first page of a related search; remember, trying to be all things to all people will only dilute your odds of success in any one category.

Look to Wikipedia: When it comes to maximizing SEO, Wikipedia might just be the most successful story on the internet. It manages to be the top search result across more than 50 percent of all searches without ever having spent a single red cent on advertising. To take advantage of this fact you are going to want to enter your niche or sub-niche into the search bar and see what specifics and categories come up.

You are then going to want to go a step further and look into the details that are provided in the overview for each of the results. The overview paragraph typically provides a summary of the article in question while also providing additional links to other potentially relevant content. With the right niche covering the right topic you could easily pull all of your keywords from this space alone.

Your own search data: While this keyword research avenue won't be too useful to start, once you manage to start drawing traffic to your page you can then look through your own search history to determine what it is that people who visit your site are looking for. This information can be found via Google Analytics where it will be broken down in several different and useful ways. This information can then be compiled with Google Correlate, which can be found at Google.com/Trends/

Correlate and can help you to take the information you have already found and expand upon it from there.

Google Correlate will allow you to figure out what topics that those who are interested in your niche are also interested in. As an example, consider a niche that focuses on exploring the great outdoors, using Google Correlate you may then discover that the target audience for exploring the great outdoors is also interested in survival preparation. Google Correlate will show you not just the keywords that are typically used in related searches, it will also tell you how often each of those related searches is performed and the percentage of total related searches it occupies. It even goes a step further and shows off the specific geographic locations that tend to use one set of keywords over another allowing you to localize your content to the specific region or regions you favor.

Look to Amazon: Once you have a general idea of the keywords that you are looking for, you can then visit Amazon.com and consider the keywords that people interested in your niche use when they are ready to buy something. As the point of social media marketing is to attract future potential buyers this is a great way to reel in potential customers who already have a buying mindset. All you need to do is to enter your niche into the search bar and see what products come up.

Finding followers

Finding followers: You will also want to create a hashtag that is specific to you and be sure to monitor it to check if other users have incorporated it. The hashtag needs to be concise, catchy, and easy enough for users to remember, while still relevant to your brand. Do your research and make sure it's not already in use so you aren't competing against someone who has already established content under the same hashtag.

You should also leverage those that are already popular. Who doesn't love #selfie or #photooftheday? Let's not forget #TBT or #MotivationMonday either. You lastly want to include hashtags that zero in specifically on your target audience. According to research published earlier this year by Simply Measured, posts with at least one hashtag see a 12.6 percent higher engagement rate than those with none.

Chapter 3: Find Your Niche

A niche market is a small and specialized chunk of a larger, more general market which, in turn, comes with a specific selection of product interests and customer demographics. To illustrate, consider the market for online dating which can then further be broken down into things such as sacred sexuality, green dating, polyamory, soulmates and more and each of these can then be further broken down into sub-categories such as soulmates over the age of 40 and gay green dating. In a world where every niche is already accounted for, sub-niches are a great place to start, though not every sub-niche is automatically going to be profitable which is where doing the right research comes into play.

When it comes to starting down the path to social media marketing, it is important to approach the process with the idea of forming a brand around the thoughts and opinions you currently hold or are interested in learning more about. Once upon a time, you could have a site that functioned purely as an aggregate of a specific affiliate marketer's products but any more, that type of site will be removed from Google search results as it does little to add new value to the Internet. This means that you will need to be marketing yourself as much as the products in question when it comes to finding success in the pay per sale or pay per lead world.

This means that when finding the right niche of products to market you need to consider more than just what the most profitable products are but also what are the ones you can put your name behind and build a brand around. One of the most common ways of doing so is by becoming an authority on the niche in question by doing lots and lots of research and then sharing that research with the appropriate types of links filtered in. Depending on the affiliate marketing potential of your hobbies, those are always a great place to start, but there are other ways to find the niche that is right for you as well.

If you find it difficult to come up with any potentially profitable niches right off the bat, then odds are you are not looking at the world around you through the eyes of a social media marketer. To do so, simply make it a point to go about your daily grind, taking notes on all of the actions you take and the conversations you have as well as anything you hear or read about. At the end of the day, all you need to do is to then sit down and find two potential niches related to every topic that you have written down. They won't all be winners, and many of them might not even be profitable, but the exercise should be enough to get the juices flowing and reveal great niche potential that was hiding in plain sight.

Another great place to find inspiration is on the longest running affiliate programs by far, Amazon.com. If you visit the site and then click on the search tab you will be given a list of all of the different types of items being sold, all of which have potential niches associated with them. What' s more, clicking on each of these options will bring up an even more specialized list of options, which, again, all have niches and sub-niches associated with them as well. After you find a few items, you can simply work backwards and determine the niche that would be interested in the items in question.

Narrow down a niche

Find a target: The first thing you will want to do when it comes time to find the right niche or sub-niche to call your own is determine who it is you are going to be targeting directly. There are several different ways you can determine your target audience, the first being the audience that you yourself are a part of. Alternatively, you can choose an audience that you have similar interests with.

If you can't seem to find an audience that speaks to you, you can instead find a niche that speaks to you and determine the audience you are going for from there. Regardless, it is important to find your audience and speak to them directly as, for example, you will find that a 25-year-old male student has very different needs, wants, and interests than a middle-aged female professional.

Consider the problems: The next thing you will want to do is take the time to really consider your target audience, or, failing that, yourself and think about any desires, aspirations, pain points, challenges, and problems that you or the group in question might have that they are going to regularly be looking to mitigate. A good way to determine if you are on the right track is if a simple Google search for the problem in question reveals plenty of blogs, websites, and forums discussing it. A problem isn't really a problem if no one is talking about how to solve it.

Find the profit: Once you have found a few problems that people are looking to solve, your next step will be to determine which are the most profitable from a marketing sense. You will want to go to Adwords.Google.com and look for the keyword planner tool. This will let you filter search results to find just those you are interested in before searching for local and global results. You will want to find the monthly searches for the topics in question, the number of searches resulting from people trying to solve the problem in question, how long those terms have been returning the results in question and how readily information about that topic already is.

Additionally, you will want to do basic searches related to the niche and make sure there are plenty of advertisers already taking advantage of the customer base. If you are having a hard time finding pages with actual advertisers, you may need to ask yourself what products you are going to actually be marketing. Taking the time to stop and think about whose products you are going to advertise at this point can be a huge resource saver in the long run and is highly recommended.

Dig deeper: In addition to understanding that a particular problem is often had by a specific group of individuals, it is important that you understand exactly what this group wants when it comes to solving a problem, for example, if you are targeting individuals looking for soulmates, you need to understand both what that means to them, how they approach love and what specifically they are looking for in a soulmate.

This portion of the process is all about going as deep as you can to learn the thought processes of the group in question but also the type of specific slang, lingo, and the language they use to describe their desires in relation to your niche. The more you know about your market, the more you can use that knowledge to create the type of ad copy and sales pitch that speaks to them specifically.

Decide if you are willing to go the distance: Once you find a niche or sub-niche that you like the look of, it is important to determine what type of content your target audience is looking for and decide if you have the ability to provide the level of quality that they are looking for. This means going the distance with the products you are endorsing every single time, and really immersing yourself in the relevant culture.

While investing in a few items that you plan on marketing might seem like a major step, the best affiliate marketers are those that create a compelling story around the items in question, and physically having the item in front of you goes a long way towards building that story. Additionally, you will want to spend the resources to acquire a high-quality digital camera and the expertise to use it properly. This doesn't mean every potential customer is looking for art in every photograph, but it does mean they are looking for quality shots, nevertheless.

Determine the number of merchants: While even the least active sub-niche imaginable has at least a few merchants who cater to it, those who are looking to build their first niche marketing site should start out in a market with a bit more variety. Your goal for multiple affiliate programs to already be in place, which will ideally allow you to set up multiple compatible compensation agreements per site.

Consider industry trends: In addition to determining the number of merchants working in the space in question, it is important to determine if the market in question has already peaked, and if so, how far in the past that peak actually was. You can use the Google tool for determining trends for this exercise and it is a great way to easily determine if a particular niche is on the way to a popularity explosion or if it went bust years before you ever started thinking about affiliate marketing. In scenarios where the biggest spike appears to have already happened, but it did so recently, then the niche in question might still have potential. Major peaks that were several years ago without a repeat performance should be avoided as a general rule.

Determine if there is a way in: In highly competitive niches there are likely a handful of websites that make up the first page of the Google search results which makes it practically impossible for anyone else to break in on the SEO front. If this is the case with a niche or sub-niche that you are considering you will want to see if there are other available avenues outside of the more traditional routes.

Prove to yourself that you have ideas for content: When it comes to deciding if you have what it takes to create a new social media marketing plan around a specific niche, it is important that you take the time to outline around 50 ideas of major content that can easily be tweaked once your pages launch. This should be different from the day to day posts that you will be generating to keep a steady flow of new commission opportunities and should be the potential types of high traffic posts that will generate new repeat visitors. This is the content that will put your site's best foot forward and you should plan on posting about 3 per week. If you can come up with 50 ideas, then several months from now you might find yourself running out of ideas.

Consider what the competition is doing: Knowing your competition and siphoning their audience is another common tactic available on Instagram. When you go to your competition's page, you can view their followers. From there, you can engage with their audience by following, liking, or commenting on their followers' posts. According to studies done by Shopify, following will produce a 14 percent follow back rate. A follow combined with a like will increase that number to 22 percent, and a follow + like + comment will garner a 34 percent follow back.

Of course, you can always expand beyond your competition's list. Browse hashtags and other popular users or photos. Put thought behind which photos you choose to like and make comments on. If you were viewing an Instagram photo and the last comment was interesting, chances are you would likely check out that account, right? Another tip to this method is to try and be the last person to comment on the photo. Utilize your emojis when appropriate and be unique.

Profitable niches to think about

If, after going through the steps above, you still haven't found the right niche, some of these evergreen options might be just the thing to set you on the road to long term affiliate marketing success.

Romance, wealth and health: When it comes to social media marketing, health, wealth and romance niches, and sub-niches are thought to be infinitely profitable because new products are always coming along for all three and the customers for each are always likely to be looking for the Next Big Thing.

- The health market includes things like medical issues, smoking cessation aids, embarrassing issues, and weight loss trends.
- The wealth market includes things like business opportunities, multilevel marketing, affiliate marketing, gambling, forex, and internet marketing

- The romance market includes things like finding a spouse, reconnecting with an ex, pick up tricks, attraction tips, and online dating.

Each of these evergreen markets has countless niches and sub-niches housed within it and countless potential customers who have already been groomed to expect a new and improved way to solve their perceived problems on a regular interval. This means there are people out there right now that are waiting for you to tell them while some new product will solve all of their problems when used properly and will be back again next week looking for something new as well.

Expensive Hobbies: Alternatively, while you yourself might not have a hobby that can be easily monetized in an affiliate marketing sense, that doesn't mean that there aren't plenty of hobbies out there with plenty of digital and physical products for the marketing. When it comes to choosing the right hobby, consider the types of things that those with lots of disposable income like to spend their time on.

Depending on the market in question, you may be able to contact merchants directly and arrange for personal demonstrations to give your content a unique touch. These types of niches are also great because there will constantly be a new stream of gear and digital products and there is also automatic content for holiday posting as a gift guide with links isn't just appreciated, it's expected.

Merchants known to pay well: While the types of niches that fall into the big payout category are typically quite competitive, that doesn't mean there isn't always going to be room for the right new person on the scene. High payout merchants include travel companies, jewelers, designer handbags, luxury watch, online casinos, a luxury boat, and car rentals as well as payday loan companies. The idea here is that it takes the same general amount of effort to generate positive advertising content for a $10 item as a $100,000 one, which in some cases may actually be true.

These types of business all tend to be recession-proof as the luxury items are targeted at those for whom money is no object, payday loans are always going to be right for someone, and gamblers are always going to need a place to gamble which online casinos are happy to provide. Again, these are not new markets which means that the competition will be fierce, if you enter into the prospect with a clear idea of just what is going to be expected, however, there is no reason you cannot find the success you seek.

Chapter 4: Create Quality Content

Picture considerations

The main ingredient of your posts on Instagram, no matter where you are sharing, is your image. Your images are the first thing that people are going to pay attention to when they land on your profile, to determine whether or not they want to follow you, see more of what you have to offer, or otherwise engage with your brand. If you want to maximize your engagement, you need to create images that are going to stop people from scrolling, keep them paying attention to you for a few moments, and hopefully result in them clicking through to your profile to learn more.

When it comes to deciding what you are going to focus your page around, the first topics you are going to want to consider are those that you are already extremely knowledgeable on or passionate about; or, barring that, something you are interested in learning much more about. This is important because you are going to be spending a lot of time with the topic between now and the point you can begin to monetize so if you don't enjoy the topic in question it is highly likely that you will run out of steam and enthusiasm for the project with literally nothing to show for it.

Taking the right types of pictures: In order to determine what types of pictures your potential followers are going to be interested in, you are going to want to visit the pages of plenty of popular individuals in your chosen niche. This doesn't mean you are going to simply want to copy what you find there, however, but instead, you are going to want to use what you find as inspiration. This will help get your creative juices flowing and make it easier to come up with the content of your own in the future. Developing your own unique perspective is crucial to being successful in the long run.

While you are on these pages, you are going to want to do more than simply lurk, instead, you are going to want to post comments on pictures you like and start interacting with the community. After all, running a successful Instagram isn't just about posting photos, it is about being a personality. Then, once people associated with the niche find your page, you won't be just another random person you will be another member of the community.

Memes: Memes in their current form have become far more ubiquitous than anyone ever anticipated. While hardly the most unique or compelling way to add a bit of visual flair to your content, they are quick, easy to make and the most popular ones have a built-in degree of popularity that can make it easy for you to seem as though you have your finger on the pulse of the internet. They are also extremely easy to make thanks to the hundreds of meme generators that can easily be found online. On the other hand, however, they aren't going to be appropriate for all audiences and the meme that you choose is inherently going to leave your posted feeling dated to a current place and time. They are best used for basic content and avoided when you are creating cornerstone content which tends to be more evergreen.

Infographics: Assuming you have the tools to create them professionally, infographics are a great way to include visual content for topics that don't naturally lend themselves to more traditional pictures and the like. Furthermore, good infographics frequently make the rounds on other blogs, increasing your market penetration exponentially.

The first thing that you are going to need to consider is what your goals are when it comes to creating the infographic in question. While improving the quality of the content you are creating is a fine reason, it is important to take the time to consider if you want to entertain your audience, educate them on the topic in question, or both. Additionally, you will want to consider the portion of your target audience you are creating the infographic for and what the general purpose of the content you are creating is going to be as well.

There are many different types of infographics including flowcharts, timelines, and visual articles which try to sum up the entirety of their related content all in one fell swoop. Regardless of the type you prefer, it is important to think about it in terms of creating a compelling narrative. This means that you want to consider the way in which the completed infographic is going to lead the user from start to finish.

Consider your content strategy

It doesn't matter what your desired niche is or how you plan on showing your passion for it. What does matter is that you choose content creation ideas that you are naturally drawn to and that you can keep up with in the long-term? Make no mistake, when you start content marketing you are getting into something that is a marathon, not a sprint, slow and steady wins the race.

Creating a small amount of content, even if it is extremely useful and well thought out content, isn't going to do much to generate the types of returns that you are looking for, it is important to choose a content creating strategy that you can stick within the long-term while also generating new content on a weekly or even a daily basis. Getting started on a content creation program and then giving up after a short period of time is even worse than not generating any content as all as when people visit your website or wherever else your content is posted and only see things that are outdated it promotes the idea that you don't care about what it is that you are promoting or that nothing new is likely to be provided which makes it less likely they will return again in the future.

To this end, it is important to generate the type of content that plays to the strengths of your brand, product, or services as well as catering to the content consumption habits of your target audience. It is important that you resist the urge to try and be all things to all people both when it comes to targeting viewers outside of your target audience as well as with the content you provide.

A poorly made piece of content isn't going to win you any new followers and may even cause some otherwise interested individuals to go elsewhere. A better choice is to instead train your target audience to expect a specific type of content from you and then work on making that content into the best version of itself that it can possibly be.

Be a leader in your field: The general idea here is that you need to do everything in your power to show that you aren't just doing what everyone else in your niche is going to be doing, if you want to generate new customers then you need to prove to them that you are ahead of the curve in whatever market you have chosen for yourself. This is accomplished by creating content that is based around the issues of the moment, getting your name out there among leading authorities that your target audience is going to recognize and getting known names to contribute their content to your site.

Create a mix of long-form and short-form content: While regular and reliable production of single-serving content such as blog posts or videos are crucial to growing your audience, you are also going to want to brainstorm options for something that is more long-form such as an eBook or a video series exploring a socially relevant topic that your target audience is sure to relate to. Social media posts are at the other end of the spectrum and can fill the role of daily content to ensure that you are never far from your target audiences thoughts.

While short-form content should strive to be as immediately relevant as possible, it is perfectly acceptable for long-form content to be of a more evergreen nature. There is no reason that you should have to constantly be updating an eBook, for example, that you created as long as you choose a topic that is likely to remain relevant to your audience for the foreseeable future. Neither do you need to rush into this type of content as a well-considered topic is going to be much more effective in pushing your brand as opposed to something that you came up within the span of just a few days?

Today's audiences are more media savvy than ever and if you didn't spend the time to create something that is legitimately worth their time they will know; and what's worse, they will make sure all their friends know not to bother with you as well. If you aren't careful, generating subpar content can be even worse than remaining silent as it can send the wrong type of message to your target audience that can be as difficult to get rid of as a particularly nasty stain on your favorite shirt.

Make a calendar and stick with it: While this is not something that you are going to need to do right away, once you are comfortable with the type of content that you are going to be creating on a regular basis as well as who your target audience for said content is, you are going to want to set a schedule for when new content is being created and stick with it. The specifics of the calendar are up to you, the crucial thing here is that you are going to want to produce content on the type of basis that your target audience can count on and that you can easily keep up with over a prolonged period of time.

While it will take weeks, if not months, for individuals to get into the habit of checking out your content on a regular basis, it will only take a fraction of the time to lose all your hard-won work. Don't let this happen to you, make it a point of only starting to create content that you can reliably produce on a regular basis.

Be prepared to track your results: The current tools that are going to be available to you when it comes to monitoring who is interacting with the content that you are providing as well as if they are sharing it with their friends, how long they are spending doing so and more are more detailed and easier to use than ever before. Unfortunately, they won't do you any good if you don't take the time to learn how to make the most of them and also to utilize them on a regular basis. Good content marketing requires quite a bit of effort and by analyzing the various types of analytics that are available for the taking you will be able to determine if your hard work is paying off.

Don't rest on your laurels, it won't do you any good to collect all the various types of data that is available to you if you don't then make an effort to utilize it as effectively as possible.

Specifically, you are going to want to be aware of which pieces of your content people are responding to most vigorously as well as that which they are avoiding like the plague. Furthermore, once you have generated a healthy amount of traffic from all of your hard work you will be able to focus in even more and determine what type of content is going to generate sales of the products or services that you are ultimately trying to sell.

With this information in hand, you will then be able to more accurately determine what type of content it is worth your time to generate and where your efforts may be better spent elsewhere. Remember, knowledge is power and analytics provide you with all the knowledge you need to be successful.

Product reviews

One of the most important types of content that you will be creating will fall under the broad category of product reviews. A review is a great way to slip in past the natural defenses that many people have against outright sales pitches as it contains practically all of the same information and none of the stigma. A review is a helpful way for customers to avoid bad products, a sales page is little more than a pushy ad. This strategy requires that you have a blog in addition to your Instagram so that you can write longer affiliate content. The pictures you post on Instagram will then act as a funnel to this type of content.

The most productive formula that many affiliates regularly use is one that looks at a specific product with a critical eye. It is important to point out any weaknesses in the product, as well as its strengths as you want your readers to assume that you are being as unbiased as possible. This means you cannot give each and every product you focus on a complete pass; otherwise, readers will not return the next time they are looking for helpful reviews. The most important part of every review post you create is to include at least two links where readers can go to find out more about the product in question, and hopefully buy it.

Broad strokes review: Depending on the type of niche you have found for yourself, you may be able to utilize simple, brief reviews that include a single picture and talk about the product as a whole for a few paragraphs before including a rating as well as a link to purchase. The goal with these types of posts is for readers to be able to quickly see which products have received the highest rating which means they are best for less expensive products which customers are typically looking for detailed information regarding.

Broad strokes reviews are effective partially because of their brevity, for more information the customer has no choice, but to click through which might be enough to get your commission, or it might even push them towards a sale. The more products that are included in each individual post the better as the goal should be to make it clear which few options are truly the best. Finally, readers are more likely to scroll through an entire page of brief reviews rather than read one that is in-depth as it appears to be a more productive use of time.

Comprehensive reviews: Depending on the type of audience you are looking for and the type of brand you are building; comprehensive reviews may be a better choice than short reviews. As the name implies, these reviews go more in depth about the product in question and are best used when it comes to food-based blogs that include a detailed explanation of the ingredients in questions all the way through the meal is finished and ready to eat. They are also useful if you have built yourself up as an authority in a specific niche for a higher priced item. You will also want to consider comprehensive reviews if, after viewing the sales page of the merchant in question you feel as though they could use a little help actually making the sale.

For less expensive or single serving items it is best to avoid this type of review as by reading the entirety of it, potential customers may not feel the need to find out more information by clicking the link in question. This is bad for two reasons, the first is that most reviews can't do as good of a job as the website for the product in question when it comes to selling effectively. Alternately, keeping your information in mind the potential customer might then go browse products and ultimately make a sale armed with your knowledge that you won't get the credit for.

Comparisons: If the product that you are marketing stands up well when compared with other similar products, you don't need to worry about writing too much about it and can instead simply compare several products based on their obvious strengths and weaknesses as well as feature parity. The best use of this type of review is when you are an affiliate for all of the products in question as there is literally no way to lose. If this is the case, then you will want to go out of your way to ensure that each product has both strengths and weakness to prevent one or two products from looking like total duds. The more types of products you include on this type of review the better, if you do it properly you can attract plenty of additional traffic simply because you are a good resource.

Negative Reviews: Many people are naturally contrarian by nature which is something you can use to your advantage when writing certain types of reviews. While you won't want to turn potential customers off to a product entirely, you should phrase the review with a negative slant. The end of the review should then include a caveat about the product only being recommended for those who are an expert in the niche in question, for only the most serious, most devoted etc. You will find that you get many extra click-throughs from people who are anxious to prove you wrong.

Catching the viewer's attention

Photos and videos are great, but captions help tell your story and captivate your audience. Strategically utilize hashtags and emojis to add another layer of interest. Tag brands in your posts if you are working with their product, and be strategic in blocking time after a post so that you are able to be thoughtful in responses to your followers.

When it comes to creating the type of content that members of your target audience are going to flock to, the caption that you use is going to be just as important as the type of content you choose to cover. Consider the following formulas to give your content the boost it needs to be successful.

Do you want to: Starting a caption with "do you want to" is a great way to get people invested in what you are writing because, assuming you know your target audience, the answer to this question is always going to be yes. As long as you already know the answer to the question then you can't go wrong with this choice.

X ways to: When a caption promises a certain number of ways to do a specific task it sets two types of specific expectations in the mind of the reader. First it promises a call to action, ideally regarding something the target audience cares about, and second, it promises choice which readers always appreciate. As such posts that follow this format are nearly 3 times as likely to be read than those that promise a single in-depth approach to solving the same problem.

Free: It doesn't matter what it is, the human brain is wired in such a way that including the word free in your caption is always going to be enough to warrant extra hits. Just be sure that you are actually giving away something free or your target audience will learn to be wary of these promises.

Avoiding duplicate content

While you will certainly be shilling for the same products as other affiliate marketers, that doesn't mean you can post the same general content that they are posting as well. Not only will this give readers little reason to prioritize visiting your page, posting content that is too similar to existing content can also hurt your ultimate search engine ranking. While you will not have to worry about dropping ranking because you posted something similar to someone else, at the same time you will not gain ranking because of duplicate posting so it should be avoided as much as possible.

This occurs because once the content has been found by the search engine on a specific page, it will omit additional instances of the same content unless it is specifically requested. This means your content will likely never be seen if it is duplicated which is why you need to do what you can to ensure that you are creating completely unique content. There are numerous free content comparison tools available online today including DuplicateContent.net.

Another important step to consider is making sure the first sentence of your caption is always unique as these are going to make it more likely your content is seen as original. Always allow for comments on your posts as well as the unique comments will help the content count as more original as well.

Hashtagging

Hashtagging on Instagram is essential. If you do not use hashtags, you can guarantee you are not reaching your audience. On Instagram, people search for hashtags of things they are interested in and then enjoy the images that have used that hashtag. If you want to be reaching as many people as possible, you need to use relevant hashtags. Ideally, you should include 10-30 hashtags on each image. Using 30 will give you the best opportunity to reach as many people as possible. Using more than 30 will result in the comment not working, as Instagram does not allow more than 30 hashtags per post.

There are two important things to remember when hashtagging your pictures: first, never put your hashtags in the caption. Always post them in the comments section. They still work, and they keep your caption clean and attractive. Second, make sure that you are not using hashtags that are too popular as you will not get seen by anyone. You also don't want to use obsolete hashtags that will barely reach anyone.

This is one place where the app PLANN comes in handy. You can type in a word that you want to hashtag and they will show you which hashtags are too popular and which ones are perfect. You can then post the ones that are best suited to reach your audience and get you seen and skip over the ones that will likely end up in your post getting buried and going unseen. While you can always use a few of the more popular hashtags, avoid using too many because you'll simply waste opportunities to reach new followers.

When you are hashtagging, a great idea is to have groups of hashtags pre-written and saved in a note on your phone. Then, you can simply copy and paste the chosen group onto the comments section of your picture within seconds of posting. This ensures that you get "engagement" (your own comment) right away. It also ensures that you begin getting interaction quickly. If the time between you posting and you receiving your first "likes" features too big of a gap, Instagram will assume you are irrelevant and you will not be seen by as many people.

Keep tabs on your hashtag once it has been created and personally thank those who interact for leaving positive comments and give genuine, personable answers to those who ask questions. Also, checking in regularly with your followers on their pages will also help drive more engagement on your page. If someone sees an interesting comment you left and found it meaningful, they are going to make their way over to your page.

Chapter 5: Finding Loyal Followers

The growth and commitment of followers is the most important part of the success of Instagram blogs; without them, you can't thrive. Consider these strategies in order to reach a larger audience on Instagram:

Schedule posts properly: Scheduling your posts can be beneficial for your blog and building your brand in the following ways:

- Organization: Scheduling your posts allows you to stay organized when dealing with your Instagram blog. Planning in advance enables you to adjust the appearance of your blogs. This will allow you to pay attention to detail with minimal time and ensure that your blog maintains the aesthetic you first established for it. You will also be able to guarantee that your posts remain consistent.

- Strategy: Instagram does not have an application feature that allows you to schedule posts. There are many online and mobile applications that you can use to plan your posts in this way, however. Many of these applications allow you to view the analysis for posts and then determine the best times to upload your posts to Instagram. Best times are classified by the times of the day when most of your followers view your posts which will ultimately lead to higher interactions. Once you know the best times for uploading your posts, you can

164

plan them out more efficiently. This is one of the easiest ways to ensure that you can draw your followers attention by knowing when they are normally online

- Convenience: Unfortunately, Instagram does not allow third-party posting, so you can't upload your posts automatically, but this shouldn't be a big problem. The planning of your posts helps you to take care of the important work in uploading content to your blog. All you have to do is post at the times you have scheduled; most applications have a callback feature that will make sure you know the time you need to post on the scheduled day. Some applications have an option that will allow you to upload from the scheduling app directly onto Instagram with a couple of steps in-between.

Use contests: Another easy way to break up the norm and gain new followers on Instagram is through contests. There are several different styles of contests, so it's up to you which one you lean towards most. Instruct entrants to tag your account in their submission, which will help get more visibility to your page.

Keep the contest simple and easy to enter, but fun. You can give away an actual prize, or feature the selected winner on your page. Having a short entry period will create a sense of urgency. If you are just starting and simply want new followers, a basic approach is the like-to-win.

If you have a pretty engaged fan base and would like to tap into their connections, the tag-a-friend method is appropriate. Do your homework and see what your competition is doing. In addition to checking out your competitors, you can also search more general hashtags like #contest or #giveaway for additional ideas (it is also a good idea to include these hashtags when you launch your promotion so others will come across it). Get creative. You want your contest to be exciting and stand out.

Like and comment on posts in your niche: In one online conference the CEO of Freshly Picked, Susan Petersen, spent some time talking about how she was able to take her Instagram account and grow it to 400,000 followers at the time (since then she has expanded her following to 800,000). Petersen states that when she was first getting started, she would spend hours each night looking through pictures on Instagram and liking them.

While this may seem like it takes a lot of work, it has worked for many other Instagram marketers in the past. Her advice for businesses and individuals who are trying to grow their reach is to go through and like about five to 10 pictures on someone else's account. It is even better if you are able to go through and leave a genuine comment on the account and even follow that person before you leave.

What this does is gets your name out there so that others are able to discover you. First, the owner of the page is going to see that you spent some time on their page, and they will want to return the favor. Then, the followers of that page will start to see your name pop up, and it may pique their curiosity. They may check out your page and even decide to follow you, growing your reach even more from a few minutes of work.

The best way to do this is to find users that are in your niche. You can do this by checking out hashtags that go with your niche or view the followers of some of your favorite names on

Instagram. However, make sure that when you do this you show some genuine personality, rather than being spammy. People can tell when you are trying to use them or spam them, and they will ignore you in two seconds if they feel like that is what you are doing.

Have a recognizable style: Having a consistent editing style will help you create some cohesivity in your feed. This makes sure that colors that are present in your photos generally look the same in every photo. Using apps like VSCO allows you to create presets so that you can use to utilize the same filter, temperature setting, contrast, highlights, etc. in every photo. This can be helpful, but it may be better to stick to editing each photo on an individual basis. This allows you to tweak different small aspects that benefit that specific photo. You can also use the filters in the Instagram app.

Photos with one of a few specific filters tend to get higher engagement than others, so using these may increase the favorability of your posts. Clarendon, Gingham, and Juno are the 3 most popular filters, followed by Lark and Mayfair. Using these filters, or similar filters from other apps can increase engagement on your photos. You can also incorporate a specific personal touch that you add to each of your photos. Some people like to post photos with an element of darkness or shadows. Doing this consistently can draw an audience that looks forward to seeing how you incorporate this element. It can narrow down the photos you are able to post, but it will help grow your following. Having one color that is present in each photo (for instance, a red shirt in one photo, a red building awning in the background of another, and a red coffee mug on a table in yet another) can be enough of an element of consistency.

Be an authority

Do the research: The first step to being seen as an authority in your niche is to do enough research that you can accurately call yourself an expert, if not the be all and end all authority on your chosen topic. The first thing this means doing is learning absolutely everything you can when it comes to the in-depth details on your niche. This means more than simply becoming familiar with the Wikipedia page on the topic, it means going to the sources that you can find connected to that Wikipedia page and then tracking down there sources as well. You will then want to do this again, and again and again until you can honestly say that you have left no stone unturned. It will unavoidably require lots of hard work and effort, though the results will certainly pay for themselves in the long run.

While learning as much as you can is always encouraged, it is important to also keep in mind the limits to what a person can realistically be expected to know and the amount of time that learning a new subject will likely take. Do yourself a favor and limit your study to just your niche or you will never feel well-versed enough to actually go ahead and start sharing what you have learned. Depending on the niche in question, you might also find it helpful to stick with a specific sub-niche that is related to the broader niche that you are working in. This can be useful if your product line focuses on a single problem as then you don't need to be the authority in your entire niche, just the authority at solving your problem. This is also a useful tactic if you find the competition for an authority figure to be too stringent when it comes to the niche as a whole.

If you are having a hard time coming up with a sub-niche to specialize in, all you need to do is turn back to Google once more and see what you get back. This will help you find a general idea of what sub-niches people consider when it comes to the niche you are broadly working in. Every niche, regardless of how narrow, has room for a sub-niche if you try hard enough, don't sell yourself short, and find the best sub-niche for you.

You will know you are ready to start putting your knowledge to good use once you can explain the most complicated parts about your niche or sub-niche in the common tongue. The goal is to not simply regurgitate well-known facts but to bring a thoughtful discussion to the niche in question. Bringing up the types of questions that everyone in the niche is asking is a great way to know you are on the right track.

While you are still learning, you may find it useful to write out a how-to guide related to the information you are researching. Studies show that teaching others is a great way to increase your own knowledge while also retaining the knowledge you are teaching more readily. It is important to do what you can to ensure the information you present is as thorough as possible as this will help you when it comes to retention, as well as to an additional authority building exercise outlined below.

Spread the word: Once you know everything there is to know about the topic in question, you are going to want to start spreading your knowledge as widely and as freely as possible, both on Instagram and beyond. You can do this by either starting your own website or by finding other experts in the niche and reaching out to them with an offer to write content for their blogs. This will then serve two purposes, first it will start to get your name out among your target audience, along with a link to your most popular Instagram post, and second it will increase your reputation among the community because another expert thought you were well-versed on the topic in question enough to give you space on their blog.

Once you get your foot in the door, you are going to want to utilize this new pseudo-celebrity as much as you can which means writing for as many niche-specific blogs as will have you. You should also go to Reddit and find all of the niche specific subreddits that you can. Your goal should be for your name to absolutely everywhere that your target audience is going to be online, no matter what. This should all include funnels back to your Instagram page that you can send potential customers too if they are interested in learning more from your wisdom on a daily basis.

Your goal in these instances is not so much to create customers, though that is always nice, rather you want to create followers who believe that you are the end all and be all when it comes to authority in your niche or sub-niche. Customers will buy things from you regularly, and maybe even leave good reviews if the mood strikes them, but followers are going to go out of their way to tell their friends about you and try and convince them to check out your content, and thus, your products. Even if they never buy anything, followers are always going to be worth their weight in conversions and should be cultivated carefully to ensure they remain as zealous as possible.

Consider your voice: Every content creator has a unique voice, a one of a kind perspective on the world that comes through in everything they do. In an extremely competitive online environment properly honing your tone can be the difference between being an authority and being just another faceless expert. You are what sets your content apart from any other, do everything you can to ensure it is unique and compelling as possible. If you aren't sure what the right voice for you is, consider the following.

- Start by making a list of the words that you feel others would use to describe you. Spend some time on each of the words that come to mind and consider how you can best make each one as clear as possible when it comes to showcasing that personality trait in the things you create.

- Add to this outline any unique speech patterns you have; this can be difficult to pick out in your own speech so it is best to get some outside input. This type of thing can be expressed in your writing in numerous ways including the sentence structure that you use, the variation of sentence style that you employ, even in how you separate your paragraphs. It is okay if you can't think of much right away, the longer you persist at writing on the regular, the more unique your content will become.

Talk yourself up: When it comes to being the authority in your field, it is important to understand that you will never truly be finished learning everything you can about your niche. Eventually, you will know who's who and it is important to make it clear to your followers that you are taking your information from credible sources. This will increase your apparent level of authority as it will make it clear that you can separate the wheat from the chaff when it comes to your area of expertise.

Before you share the sources of the information you are iterating upon, it is important to vet them thoroughly to ensure everything is as valid as it first appears. For starters, this means having a clear idea of just who created the content you are planning on referencing including their general level of authority in the niche. Reliable sources can be easily verified and you will want to know everything about the names you choose to associate with, past and present, before you go ahead and put yourself out there. This means it is just as important to see who the authority currently spends their time associating with, and what their Twitter feed looks like. While this may seem like a lot of effort, it is important to keep in mind that linking yourself to the wrong people can easily kill your brand before you even get it fully established.

Write a book: Assuming you have done all of the recommended research, you should now have more than enough knowledge to put together an eBook on your topic that is anywhere from 10 to 20 thousand words. If that seems like a lot, consider the how-to guide you wrote as part of your researching phase and think of it as a detailed outline of what you can include in your book. The idea might be intimidating, but if you consider how much writing you have already done for various blogs, you'll find that the total word count is a lot less scary than it might have initially seemed.

If you don't have the time or inclination to write a book of your own, you can instead hire a freelance ghostwriter for the rate of approximately $1 per 100 words which means that you can have a 10,000-word book written for $100 or fewer thanks to freelancer writer marketplaces like UpWork.com. Either way, you will likely want to hire a professional graphic designer to create the front and back covers for your book as having a professional looking book will increase your authority proportionally. This will likely cost about the same, if not a little more than having the book written would cost.

The end goal is to post the book to the Kindle Marketplace, which you can do for free, Amazon then takes a portion of each sale depending on the price of the book, but for your purposes, you will likely be most frequently giving the book away for free. Once you have the finished product you can then include a link to it and instead of selling followers the book you then promise to give it to them for free if they agree to sign up for your email newsletter list, the specifics of which are discussed in the next chapter. This will give you access to valuable statistics related to your followers and also your target audience while at the same time doing more to convince them you are the true authority on the topic. After all, you wrote the book on it.

Chapter 6: Converting Your Followers

Producing a constant stream of relevant, quality content, and doing everything in your power to ensure that it is the type of information that your target audience is interested in, is a crucial part of a successful social media marketing campaign. However, creating content isn't the end goal, of course, and when you get down to it, is really just a means to an end and that end is conversions. You can have the best content in your niche, but if you don't take the time to maximize your conversions, your commission rate is going to be nowhere near your total views.

Luckily, research has shown that users to are on Instagram are inclined to spend $65 per sale, while users on Facebook spend $55 and only $46 is spent on Twitter. Additionally, posts on Instagram tend to have a conversion rate of 1.85 percent, second to Facebook's conversion rate of 1.08 percent. However, Instagram exceeds Twitter where the conversion rate is 0.77 percent and Pinterest at 0.54 percent. Consider the following tips to ensure you can meet or beat the average.

Determine your goals: First and foremost, it is important to understand that there is more to a successful marketing campaign than simply bringing the right type of people to your page. You may be interested in generating a higher rate of brand mentions, improving your social media mentions, improving your search engine ranking, improving your email newsletter metrics, generating sales leads or just improving your website traffic to generate additional advertising revenue.

It doesn't matter what your goals are, you are going to need to track your results properly if you hope to gain any traction.

Luckily, there are metrics that can be used to track your goals, whatever it is that they might be. If you are looking to track the number of times your website is mentioned elsewhere, then you are actually looking to track a metric known as voice share which can be done with a free tool called Social Mentions which compares your overall mentions to others in the same niche. If you are looking to improve your search engine results, then there are plenty of SEO tools that can help you track your rank in real time.

Create customer personas: While effective social media marketing speaks directly to a specifically targeted audience, if you are looking to maximize the conversions of the content you create there is still more you can do to be even more specific. The secret to doing so effective is to create what is known as customer personas which will segregate the customer base into easy to target chunks based on things like lifecycles, purchasing patterns, emotions, behavioral motivations and more.

In order to use customer personas to their fullest potential, you will need to take advantage of all of the data you have hopefully been gathering from your users. Look back through it and see what types of patterns emerge, these are the characteristics it will be helpful to give extra focus to. You will really want to strive to be as precise as possible during this process which means you will need to keep an eye out for points where you can segment your audience that are mutually exclusive from one another. Things like location, age, and gender are all fine starting places but you will need to find more actionable characteristics if you want your customer personas to be as effective as possible. Questions you should ask of your users include things like:

- What about their lifestyle impacts their buying choices?
- Who makes the decision in the households my users live in?
- What might cause them to start using the competition instead?
- What are their tastes and preferences?
- What are their goals and dreams?
- What are their precise demographics?

One of the reasons that customer personas are so useful is that they can make it easier to remember that each set of numbers in the metrics you are looking at is an actual person with real dreams, hopes, and goals. They make it easier to look at your users as individuals which, in turn, makes it much less difficult to understand their unique buying habits, especially when it comes to walking away from an uncompleted purchase. This level of deeper communication can then ultimate make it easier for you to generate the type of content that they are looking for and will respond positively too.

Increase engagement

An easy way to increase your engagement is by posting when your followers will see it. In a study conducted by Forrester, 11.8 million user interactions on posts made by 249 branded profiles were analyzed to find that top brands are posting on average 4.9 times per week. Every niche and target audience is unique, so it might take some research on the front end and a bit of work and planning, but it is well worth it since posting and scheduling tools are available to you at no cost. Knowing your audience and when they are online is especially important since the change of Instagram's algorithm moved away from chronological and now gives priority to the posts with the most engagement.

Start increasing engagement through regramming. Use high-quality content that is consistent with your look and feel and supports your brand. When a fan receives a personal shout-out from you it will only strengthen their engagement and encourage them to continue following and could quite possibly turn into a brand ambassador for you. You turn a somewhat emotionless connection into a meaningful one while cross-pollinating your Instagram accounts. In seeing this, other fans will be motivated to submit great content and voila, you yourself have even more great content and supporters.

Maximize your conversion rates

The ultimate goal of everything you post on your site should be to sell viewers on a specific merchant's products. As such, it is important to formulate your postings in such a way that they ensure you convert as many viewers as possible to paying customers.

Phrase the content properly: As previously discussed, one of the best ways of doing so is to make the posting appear personal, a personal story on your page is worth a closer look when a more generic ad simply won't cut it. Additionally, it is important to always include the type of person the product in question is for, this will make people who are that type of person take interest because it says the product was created with them in mind. Assuming the group in question has a positive association, you will also attract people who want to be identified in that way.

State, don't imply, the benefits of the product in question: A recent study found that simply by listing 5 bullet points related to the benefits of using their service, a major online booking website was able to increase their conversion rate by nearly 200 percent. While you might feel as though you are elucidating on the benefits of the product you are discussing, it turns out that people really like it when the benefits are stated as bluntly as possible. While you might not experience a 200 percent increase in conversions, you will likely notice a real difference.

The benefits you are talking about don't need to be revolutionary or even that far outside of what is expected, the most important thing, however, is that whatever benefits you list have to be true and easily verifiable. For example, the online booking site listed its benefits as being easy to use, 100 percent secure, guaranteed, free from excess charge and promised to have always available customer service. It doesn't matter that these are the types of things customers expect from this type of service, simply seeing it reiterated upon is enough to make a difference.

Avoid ad fatigue: Running the same ad for too long can become tiresome for your audience, and they will stop responding to it. You can experiment with different time periods, but changing your ad completely or changing the offer every week or two could help with ad fatigue. You do not want your audience to begin ignoring your ads, because they think there is nothing new for them to discover, so find new ways to excite your audience. Using humor, video, or an irresistible sale every so often can help reenergize your ad, if you are sensing ad fatigue.

Match your tone to your brand: The tone of your ads should match the existing tone of your brand. For example, if you used "luscious locks" to refer to your hair care products, then this terminology should be made apparent in your Instagram ad for those hair care products too. You must post regularly and remain active on your social media platform. A constant and consistent flow of content is how your audience knows you're still in business, and how they keep up to date on your latest, exciting business offerings.

Use what Instagram has to offer: Instagram has got some unique offerings, including Layout and Boomerang, two exciting features which offer businesses a unique opportunity to present and show their products in exciting new ways. Experiment with it and see how you can use it to your brand's advantage.

Picture before you post: Stop and have a think about how your ad is going to look on a mobile phone. Instagram is a heavy, mobile-first experience platform, which means that almost (if not all) your viewers will be seeing your content first and foremost on their mobile devices. Picture how your ad is going to look like on these devices and see if there's anything else you could do to optimize it before you submit your post. Are your images the right size? Is the video aspect ratio according to specifications? Did you remember to include closed captions?

Put your call to action in the spotlight: The best way to get people to take action is to get them to sit up and pay attention. If your ad has got a call to action, put it right smack in the middle of your video where it's going to be hard to miss. This is also great for capturing the attention of already interested viewers who are engaged and watching your video. Call to actions at the start of videos only had a 3.15 percent conversion rate, while the call to action placed at the end of videos were at 10.98 percent.

Utilize Google AdSense

By taking advantage of Google's advertising program you can take advantage of every single individual who visits your site via impression based targeted advertising. Additionally, if you include a search bar that works for the entirety of Google then any purchases that come from that search bar will be credited as your commission as well. This is a particularly useful feature if you are fond of comprehensive reviews as it can be a way to mitigate the fact that people tend to leave a comprehensive review without clicking through to a merchant site.

The first thing you will want to consider is the types of block formatting available to find the one that will best fit your site. According to Google, 160x600, 300x250, and 336x280 are the shapes that routinely see the best results. It is important to stick with a color scheme for the ad in question that doesn't immediately contrast with the rest of your site. The location you choose for the advertising is also important as if the potential customer sees the ad too quickly they could easily be turned off from your site completely. As such, the far left or right of either sidebar or in the footer are generally considered the least intrusive placements.

If you are interested in giving AdSense a try, you can download a plugin to set it up easily from the plugin installation menu where you traditionally add new add-ons. Search for the Google AdSense plugin and choose the option to install. Once the plugin has been installed you simply find the plugin list and choose the option to activate AdSense. You will then need to visit the plugin settings menu and chose the option to Get Started.

You will need to start by signing into your Google Account, from there you will need to check the information it can find regarding the site in question. Assuming everything is correct you will want to click the option to Verify. Once your account has been verified you will need to go back into the plugin settings to activate it. You can set up automated ads for both the mobile and primary versions of your site. Once you have turned on AdSense you can manage the placement of your ads by using the Manage Ads option found in its settings.

The next step is to choose the template that you want to add the ads to, each template can have a different set of advertisements. You will want to Review the template in question by finding the relevant option near the Design button. This will show you a preview of the template in question with green boxes placed where the ads will ultimately go. You can place new AdSense boxes, 3 maximum, by dropping markers in specific places or delete existing AdSense boxes by selecting the X next to their locations. Save and you are ready to start profiting from impressions.

Chapter 7: What to Sell

Physical products

FBA: Fulfilment by Amazon (FBA) is often considered a subset of drop shipping, though there are some significant differences as well. For example, whereas with standard drop shipping, the third party is responsible for the fulfillment of the order as well as sourcing the products, with FBA you find the products you are interested in selling yourself and send them to Amazon who then takes care of a majority of the work after that in exchange for a portion of the overall profits when the item sells.

In addition to making the transaction part of the equation easier, FBA members also get preferential treatment when it comes to search results so their items show up ahead of other similar items from merchants who are not a part of the FBA service. What's more, FBA members' items are all eligible for Amazon Prime free two-day shipping which is a huge bonus when compared to other items that don't qualify. As such, simply by signing up for the program you are already ensuring that your products have a significant advantage over the competition even if they cost a little more or you are just starting out so your seller rating isn't as high as it might otherwise be.

FBA works by having sellers send their items to the nearest FBA fulfillment center where the products are then stored, for a small fee based on space requirements, until they are sold.

Amazon also offers labeling or preparation services for an additional fee. Then, when a customer finds your item and decides to pull the trigger, Amazon then takes care of all the shipping, customer service, and potential hassles related to returns as well. In addition to making the entire process of selling items easier to get started with, having the Amazon name directly attached to your product helps significantly when it comes to customer mindshare. Studies also show that FBA seller products typically sell as much as 30 percent faster compared to similar products listed by non-FBA sellers.

In return for these benefits, FBA members pay $40 per month along with a sales percentage and fees related to the weight of the item when it comes to shipping and handling along with storage fees. While this might make the program less attractive to those who are dealing with larger items, if you are selling smaller, lighter items then this is definitely going to be worth it.

Stick to a niche: Before you set up your Amazon store, and even before you start buying products, it is important to have a clear idea who the market for these products is going to be. Finding the right customers to focus on will allow you to more accurately choose the products that appeal to them and avoid wasting time and money storing items at the FBA fulfillment center that are never going to sell. The best niches are those that are currently underserved on Amazon which means you are going to want to take a look at products that have only a few different options as opposed to dozens, or even hundreds. Once you have a clear idea of who you are going to be selling to, it makes it much easier to find cheap products that fit the bill.

T-shirts

If you want an evergreen source of passive income, then you can sell t-shirts online to your customers. People have been buying t-shirts online for a long time. Now you can sell these t-shirts but allow customers to choose a design that they like.

To succeed in this particular venture, all you will need are designing skills and some marketing skills. One of the benefits of selling t-shirts or other similar products is that you can get others to do the hard work for you. You will not need to print a single t-shirt or mail the printed t-shirt to a customer because all this is handled by other people.

So you will receive orders from customers, process the orders online, and let others do the rest. In the process, you get to earn a decent reward. The key to success in this line of business is providing variety and convenience to your customers. It is one of the best and simplest ways of generating an income even when you are away engaged in other matters.

Getting started: You will need to come up with designs and then make use of Print-On-Demand affiliate programs. Customers who visit your website will take a look at the t-shirts you have displayed and the designs available then choose both a t-shirt and a design.

1. Get your own online store: The first step you need is to design your own store. It is here that your customers will come to purchase the t-shirts. Therefore, ensure that your online store is presentable and professionally designed. You can always get a professional to design the store for you.

It is much better to have your own store where you are completely in charge, and there are no additional fees and charges apart from the hosting charges, Internet costs, and other standard costs.

It should have all the essential features of a store such as s shopping cart, t-shirt displays, a checkout counter, contact information, and all the others. You can get a professional web design firm to create your online store.

If you want, you can get a store on the popular site shopify.com. This store provides entrepreneurs a chance to create their own store for drop shipping business. However, they charge you a monthly fee whether you make money or not.

2. Have a number of great t-shirt ideas: When customers come to your store, they will be looking to purchase interesting, unique, fun, and probably catchy t-shirts. This means you will have to come up with lots of designs for them to choose from. It is your creativity here that is really bringing in the customers. Therefore, ensure that you provide a good number of t-shirt designs for your customers.

Sometimes your customers will request personalized or customized t-shirt designs. While these may not be the norm, you should be flexible enough to approve such requests. And you should feel free to request additional payment for the special request.

Always focus on a niche market rather than the entire market. Focus on what you are good at and produce designs for that particular niche. Remember that those who try to please everyone ends up pleasing no one.

3. Put in time up-front: If you want your t-shirt printing business to thrive, you will need to put in some time, especially in the early days. For instance, you will need to be there during the design and setup of the website, you will have to provide content as well as write the texts, and so much more.

    If you put in the time in the initial days, then you will not have to work so hard once the business starts to pick. For instance, you should come up with most of your t-shirt designs as early as possible so that they are ready once the store opens.

    Initially, you may have to put in 10 – 30 hours to get your online store up and running

4. Identify a t-shirt printing partner: To be successful in this business, you will need to partner with a renowned t-shirt designing drop-shipping company. There are a number of these companies available. One of these is Printful. These companies will receive orders from you and process the orders then mail the printed t-shirts to the buyers.

    The print-on-demand companies have a wide variety of t-shirts to choose from. They range in size, color, and texture, therefore, ensure your customers get this variety too. You can always open a free account with them whenever you want. Then once you are ready, you may place your orders.

There are plenty of benefits for signing up with Printful. For starters, it is free to open an account. Once you have an account with them, you can then connect seamlessly with the company and place orders as you receive them.

You can receive affordable t-shirt samples which you can then display on the website for your customers. The firm offers white labeling services. This means that they label packages with your address, so clients understand that the t-shirts came from your store and nowhere else. You may print more than just t-shirts with these print companies. Other items that can be printed include dresses, sweatshirts, tank tops, and many others.

Digital products to sell

Start a webinar: Creating an online series of courses or a webinar is a great way to make money online if you are a master of a skill that you know other people would be willing to pay to learn. After you have confirmed that your skill has value to others, all you need to do is to record yourself doing the skill in a teachable fashion and then post it online where others can pay for the privilege of learning from you. It is important to keep in mind that not every skill is easily marketable, however, keep the following tips in mind in order to ensure you are producing content that other people will actually be willing to pay for and be able to utilize themselves.

If you like the idea of creating a webinar but aren't sure if you have the right set of skills, the best thing to do is to make a list of all the skills you possess. You will then want to go through it one by one and remove those that you do not feel comfortable discussing in detail. Remember, in order to get people to pay to learn from you it is important the information you provide is more than what they could simply learn online with a quick Google search. If you can't go deep on the topic in question you are going to want to keep looking.

Depending on the topic you decide on, you might be able to do a simple lecture or narrated PowerPoint presentation. If you are going to be going through the steps of some complicated skill then a video where you go through the steps one by one is probably the way to go. Regardless of how you choose to present the content, it is important to have a high-quality video and audio stream. This means you are going to want to invest in low-level professional equipment which will likely run you between 300 and 500 dollars.

While this cost might seem steep at first, the quality of your results will make it easier for you to turn a profit, so the equipment will pay for itself in time. The quality of the content you produce is of the utmost importance. If the quality isn't there then word will spread to that effect and the first round of paying customers you attract will end up being your only round of customers. Remember, you will only have one chance to make a good first impression, don't blow it.

Sell stock photos: If, after getting started with Instagram you find that you have a knack for taking photos, then a great way to double dip is to sell images of items in your niche to stock photo sites. There are numerous different website out there that will purchase pictures from aspiring photographs including Shutterstock.com and iStockPhoto.com. These sites, and others like them, allow photographers to post their work for free in exchange for a portion of the profits. Typically, the range of their cut is between 50 and 85 percent of the total made per picture with more accomplished photographers getting to keep more of their money. As such, it is important to look at selling stock photos as a numbers game where quantity beats out quality. Consider the following tips to ensure you sell as many pictures as possible.

The bigger stock photo sites are very particular about who they let into their marketplace which means your pictures are going to need to be up to snuff. This means you are going to want to use something more than your smartphone to take the pictures with. Additionally, before you submit anything you are going to want to blow it up as large as possible and check for flaws as you will only get one chance with these sites to make the right sort of "first impression."

Before submitting anything, you are going to want to look through what is on display for the site you choose and find a type of picture that is popular enough to have its own section, but not so popular that you are going to have to fight with hundreds of other photographers in order to have a shot of being chosen. In well-defined genres, the most popular photographers have already laid claim to the first few pages of results which means you are going to have to fight extra hard if you want to break into a spot where someone is likely to actually see your pictures.

After you have been accepted to a site, it is important that you provide the right labels to ensure your pictures get seen by interested buyers. This means you are going to want to label them accurately based on content, but also include a few uses for the picture that could be considered outside of the box. Coming up with unique uses for your pictures will help them stand out amidst search results that largely turn up subtle variations on the same thing over and over again. This is not to say that you should put your pictures in completely unrelated categories, however, as if your pictures show up too frequently then repeat clients will stop paying attention to them completely.

These stock photo sites always have a free section where photographers can post their work free of charge. It is important to always have a few pictures in these sections as it will help prospective customers get to know your work, even if they aren't paying for the privilege. If a customer likes your free pictures, the next time they are in the market for paid work it is more likely that they will think of you first.

Writing the book: If you like the idea of selling products online, but don't want to deal with the hassle of actually stocking products or running your own online store, then getting into the eBook game might be the right choice. Amazon's Kindle marketplace has been selling more eBooks than the physical book market since 2012 and the number of eBooks sold per year is only increasing. What's more, adding books to the marketplace is free, Amazon simply takes a cut of each sale.

When it comes to deciding what your eBook is going to be about, the most frequently purchased books tend to be in either the self-help or how-to genres. People who purchase these types of books are always looking for the "next big thing" in their favorite topic which means they are already conditioned to prefer newer books to older ones just because they are new. What's more, many of these topics don't change all that much from year to year, effectively making them evergreen, assuming they don't go into a lot of time and place specifics.

In general, you are going to want to choose a topic that is simple enough that people will feel comfortable getting all of their details from an eBook, but not so simple that they could easily look up all of the details via a simple Google search. What's more, you are going to want to your best to put a somewhat unique spin on the topic in question to help to set it apart from the crowd. The best way to find this spin is to look at the books currently at the top of the charts for your chosen topic and then look for an angle that is not currently being represented.

If you are well-versed in a particular skill, topic, or theory, then you can write your own eBook using any of the templates that are widely available online for free. The average eBook is between 10 and 15 thousand words and a majority are based on a beginner level explanation of the topic or are an overview of the various aspects of it (such as this book). What this means is that you don't actually need to have a deep understanding of what you are writing about in order to produce the type of content that is going to sell.

Once the book is written, there are numerous free sources that will format it for the Kindle Marketplace and anyone with access to Photoshop can put together enough of a cover to work for your purposes. If you know your stuff you can produce an evergreen form of passive income with only a few day's work.

If, however, you are interested in getting into the eBook game with as little time and energy as possible, or if you are planning to go hard on the strategy with numerous books at once, then you may want to find someone else to do your writing instead. There are countless eBook writing services available online, but to get the best value you are going to want to reach out to writers directly. The best way to go about doing so is to visit task sourcing websites such as UpWork.com and signing up for a free account.

Sites like this allow those with writing jobs to connect with writers, at a rate that is typically around $1 for 100 words which means a 10,000-word book can be written for $100. The fees for using the site are then taken out of the writer's pay so you don't need to pay anything for using the site to find a writer. All you need to do is create a job listing with the details of the book you are interested in writing and then let the writer's come to you. The end result will be edited professionally and all you will need to do is to format it for Kindle.

You can then find someone to format it for you and also create a cover using the site Fiverr.com whose claim to fame is that all of their users are ready to do your job for you for just $5.

Once you have a book that is ready to be posted to the Kindle Marketplace, all you need to do is to create a seller account and then choose the price that you are willing to sell the book for. Remember, quantity is going to outweigh the quality of each individual sale and the cheaper your book is, the more likely that someone is going to buy it, especially early on when you don't have any reviews. For books that are priced between $2.99 and $9.99 Amazon takes 70 percent of the profits from each sale but only 35 percent of those that are priced lower or higher than this spectrum.

What this means, is that you are actually going to see a higher return on your investment by pricing your book at $1.99 than you would at $2.99 by approximately 10 cents per sale. While this might not seem like much, given the sheer number of eyes on the Kindle marketplace every day, a few thousand sales, even for new books from unknown authors, isn't unrealistic. Additionally, the cheaper price point will make your book seem as though it has a greater value compared to books of a similar length that are priced higher.

Books with positive reviews tend to receive more sales which means that in order to maximize your profit you need to get your book out in front of people who are likely to leave reviews. If you already have your own website dedicated to a niche that includes the book you have written then giving it away to visitors who sign up for your newsletter allows you to kill 2 birds with one stone. This will allow you to provide value in exchange for customer details, while also ensuring that they are more likely to leave reviews because they are committed to your site enough to provide their information. Alternatively, you can reach out to influencers in a field related to the topic you have chosen and send them a copy for free in hopes that they will leave a review.

Tips for success

Whenever possible, the product you are attempting to sell should be something you are familiar with and, quite frankly, have a passion for. This will help you a great deal when it comes to researching and understanding quality standards, manufacturing practices, pricing, and in particular when following up from a customer service perspective. If your product is one that you are intimately familiar with, and use regularly as a consumer, then you are in a great position to be an advocate for, and with your customer.

Everything from your pricing, to shipping and quality expectations will be measured against your own high standards, enabling you to most likely exceed the expectation of even your most discriminating customer. Not to mention the fact that when dealing with potential suppliers, an educated consumer is always in a better position to negotiate. There will always be products out there that you are interested in offering on your site because of a high demand, and strong margins, but you know little about them. The point here is that you can certainly pursue those products, and should if the math makes sense. But do not do so blindly. Become educated very quickly and understand the product inside and out before you commit to selling it.

Next, do your homework. Research the marketplace in relation to the product, or products you want to sell. Are the customers readily available? Is there an adequate demand for the product? Is there profit in the product? In other words, if you are attempting to move a product like reading glasses, you should probably look at the margins closely and decide whether or not you want to jump into the competition pool with Lenscrafters and Americas Best Eyewear. Those brands are pretty consistently offering ridiculous deals like $65 for two pairs of prescription glasses. You likely cannot compete with that, so why try?

These are two very large brands that use lost leader offers like this and can afford to because they make their own product in house or have very low margin deals cut with suppliers based on volume, and their real objective is to get consumers into their physical sites, where they actually make their money. You simply cannot play ball on that field, nor should you want to.

Once you have zeroed in on your product line, let's get back to the original question...who are you going to sell it to? And further, how do you get them to your storefront?

As you begin to put together your marketing strategy, you must also consider, what value you will add to the product. What will the consumer get from you that they would not have gotten from the other guy? Often times, sellers get hung up on price and make that their main selling point. While that strategy may work for companies like Walmart, it will not work for you in the dropshipping world, if great pricing is all you have to bring to the table.

Anyone can sell stuff cheap. In order to be effective, and successful, you have to stand out from the crowd. You will likely enter the business thinking you are just going to sell things. When in fact, when you succeed, it will be because you realize that you are a retailer that offers solid products, at competitive pricing, but most importantly you are a reputable company that offers innovative solutions and world class customer service to your customer base.

You are open to any input they have and are available at any turn to help them through a purchasing decision, or rectifying what they might feel was a bad purchasing decision. These are the value ads that will differentiate you from the completion out there.

Chapter 8: Use Instagram as a Sales Funnel

As already discussed, turning a profit from all of your hard work requires conversions and to do that you need to focus on turning your Instagram page into what is known as a sales funnel. That requires a process or funnel that will help you convert inquiries into customers. Instagram provides you an advanced feature that allows you to get ultra-specific about your ad targeting. That makes getting in front of the RIGHT people, at the right time, extremely effortless.

No matter where your customer is in their buying journey, you can rest assured that there is an advanced feature that can help you to put your product and service in front of them at the right time.

Top of the funnel: The top of any good social media sales funnel are the followers that make the entire process possible. The more followers you have in the top of the funnel the more sales you will ultimately generate in the long-term. Social media marketing is a numbers game, plain, and simple which means that the more followers you can entice with the tips discussed in the previous chapters, the more people you can entice to your site, and the more sales you can ultimately generate.

This is also why growing your followers from your target audience is so important. One topic not covered in this book is buying followers which will ultimately result in dead weight as if they aren't part of your target audience then they won't be swayed by your advertising and won't buy anything as a result.

Funnel middle: While having a large following has a variety of benefits all on its own, it is really only the first step when it comes to creating a successful sales funnel, you will still be required to interact with them and tell them what to do by clearly demonstrating your value. Luckily, keeping your existing audience engaged is easier than growing a new follower count from scratch as long as you continue to develop content that you know they are going to like. You will know that you are on the right track when you can see an engagement rate of five percent or more. Keeping up with both new and existing users are bound to feel pretty exhausting at times, but it is crucial to being able to keep your funnel moving along effectively.

Bottom of the funnel: The bottom of the funnel is filled with the members of your target audience that are going to be the most likely to purchase your goods or services. You can pinpoint these individuals before they purchase anything because they are the ones who are always engaging in your posts and commenting on your pictures. Nevertheless, they won't make a purchase without being prompted which means you want to take special care to get them to wherever you need them to go in order to make a purchase.

You are going to want to have multiple different sales pages ready and waiting so that different posts can link to different versions that are perfect for different audiences. Additionally, it is important that your landing page is mobile-optimized for obvious reasons.

While certain niches will have success with links leading directly to sales pages, others will have far better luck extending the conversation with followers out even further and instead send them to a landing page that allows them to sign up for your email mailing list. While making conversions via Instagram is one thing, getting followers onto your mailing list virtually ensures they will spend more in the long-term. The easiest way to get those in the bottom of the funnel to sign up for your mailing list is to offer an Instagram only offer as part of the deal, that is tailored to your target audience for maximum effect.

Assuming your set your bio link to your email mailing list landing page, you will want to ensure that the posts that point followers towards it include a strong call to action to avoid any confusion on the part of your followers. Remember, when it comes to social media marketing clearly stating things is always the right choice.

You will then want to track the results of your individual sales campaigns to see which are the most successful. The easiest way to do so is to simply purchase a new domain name for each campaign so that you can easily track the clicks that each receives via Google Analytics. As the domain name that you will ultimately be using will be shortened to a bite-sized URL the specifics don't matter, keeping the costs on this option from growing out of control.

Alternately, another viable solution is to generate what is known as UTM parameters to attach to your primary URL. These parameters are made from small portions of code that are added to the end of an existing URL to make it trackable to Google Analytics.

You can see everything after the main URL ends is part of a UTM structure. Typical UTM parameters include Source, Medium, and Campaign (name). These are all trackable in Google Analytics under Acquisition.

In the case of tracking an Instagram post, you should use.

- utm_source=Instagram
- utm_medium=Post
- utm_campaign=Unique identifier for your campaign

RavenTools.com offers a free UTM link generator to help you get started.

The downside to these types of URLs is that they tend to look messy if left untended, which means you will want to utilize bit.ly or a similar service to generate a serviceable URL. From there, when followers click on the link you provide you will be able to track the campaign for research purposes in the future.

Once you have that mechanism in place, you, then have to ask yourself: how am I going to get people to sign up for the mailing list? There are a lot of different routes that you can take for this specific purpose, but the most obvious is just to simply ask them. Some people make it a lot more complicated, and we'll get into that in just a second, but there's absolutely no harm in straightforwardly having a box to the side of the webpage where people can enter their email address and sign up for the mailing list. This is an easy way for your users to keep in touch with you and keep up to date on your most pertinent posts, so if they like your site, there's no chance that they'll miss out on your posts.

However, there are a few other options you can take. It's pretty easy to set up scripts that will "gate" content if people don't join your mailing list. This is a good way to turn people away from your site, but if you set the floor high enough – maybe 10 posts before people are asked to sign up – then you can avoid ostracizing people who aren't interested and get the email addresses of the people who are. Moreover, you can do something simple like set up a pop-up box that will ask people to enter their email address and join the mailing list, with an obvious way to leave the box and continue browsing if they choose to do so. This shouldn't upset too many people, as most users understand that mailing lists can be one of the most efficient and important ways for an enterprising entrepreneur to keep up with their customers.

Tips for success

Know your low hanging fruit: If you don't know who your ideal customer or "low-hanging fruit" is, you can't provide ensure they will take to the funnel. That includes your ads. Not just your posts and blog posts. While demographics like where they live and what gender they are, are nice, they aren't enough in today's competitive marketplace to drill down and be specific to who you can help.
It just is not a strong enough call to action or desire, to guarantee any form of commitment or action on their part. There is no WIIFM moment. (What's in it for me). You need to sit down and figure that out for each of the audiences you serve.

Target your content creation: As previously mentioned, not every buyer is the same and not every buyer as at the same buying stage in their individual buying journey. The content you create in this initial step needs to be segmented. For example, if you are trying to go after chiropractors, and lawyers and dentists, each of those professions has their own set of routines, habits, needs and most importantly language or way of communicating with peers and others. As long as it is most relevant to your audience and you remain consistent then you are already off to a winning strategy.

Directly driving people to your website means that you make one post and it immediately sends people through to your website so that they can start shopping with your brand. You do this anytime you make a post that encourages people to go to the link in your bio and start shopping for the product or service that you were talking about in your post. You can also have the same impact by sending people to your link through your stories or through your IGTV channel. As long as you are directly asking someone to go to your link, you are directly channeling them through your funnel. This means that indirect funnels will have a direct element since at some point you are going to need to bounce people from your Instagram profile to your website.

Indirect sales funnels are a great way to provide your audience with plenty of information before they leave your page to check out your website, as you have directed them to. Since you are driving them through two or three posts, you are able to provide plenty of diverse insight and information on your product, service, or brand before they ultimately land on your website. There are many different ways that you can drive people around your Instagram profile, depending on what it is that you are trying to accomplish and what type of content you have to offer.

For example, you can encourage someone watching your story to go check out your post, and then when they check out the post you can have a piece written that encourages them to check out your latest IGTV video, and then that video can lead people to your website. You can also have one post that directs people to your website and then use your stories, IGTV, and live video feed to drive everyone over to that story first, where they read your content before then clicking over to your website.

Once on your website, your leads should quickly be able to determine who you are, what you value, and what you have to offer. Then, there should be a clear and easy way for them to either learn more about you or discover what you have to offer. Your website should be built in a way that walks your leads through the process of landing on your website, learning about you, and then browsing and purchasing your products. You should also have a newsletter capture on your website so that if people land on your page but do not purchase from you, they can still input their email if they want and receive updates and a reminder to come shop with you at a later time. This way, they remain in the funnel until they either choose to exit or they choose to purchase one of your products.

Leverage Your Existing Community: Using your existing community to help you build your account is a great opportunity to really get your name out there and grow your account quickly. You can leverage your followers by encouraging them to share your images by tagging their friends in them or by sharing them to their stories. You can also use giveaways or contests as a way to encourage more followers to follow you, as they will want to follow you to stay posted on your giveaway results.

Utilize Instagram Shopping: As you might expect from the name, Instagram shopping is a means for brands to tag specific products that appear in their pictures with prices and names. From there, all it takes is for a user to tap on a photo for them to be taken to a product description page which ultimately leads them to the sales page. In order to take advantage of this funnel opportunity, you will need to also have an active Facebook business page as well as a Facebook Shop.

Chapter 9: Social Media Principles

Don't overdo it: The first thing you need to keep in mind is don't include affiliate products in every post. Think about it like this: you may have your car salesman neighbor show up to your door wanting to chat for a bit, or you may have a vacuum cleaner salesman show up to your door. Both will show up to your door, but which do you want to invite in?

Even if you know that your car salesman neighbor is going to egg you on a bit with a couple of jokes about coming out and getting a new car (and perhaps maybe even convincing you), you know that you'll also have a few laughs and generally have a good time with them. Meanwhile, the vacuum cleaner salesman comes for one reason and one reason alone: to try to sell you something. The entire time, you're trying to be impressed; you never let your guard down; you're thinking critically about every last thing that they say trying, subconsciously, to find ways to talk yourself out of purchasing whatever they're throwing at you.

The thing is that when you include affiliate marketing products in every post, it's fairly obvious that you're trying to get people to click on it. Even if they have no idea what affiliate marketing is, they probably have heard of people including links in their posts or doing posts specifically to promote a product. That's great, but it doesn't make them want to click the product. Moreover, it makes them even less likely to return to your site, because they subconsciously feel like they're just going to have sales offers lobbed in their face. They're not wanting that.

They're searching for something to buy related to your niche – they're looking to know more about it, first and foremost.

Remember always that if somebody could get the same asset or information from you for free that you are otherwise trying to sell them, they absolutely would. They aren't on the internet trying to buy things; they're on the internet trying to see what insights they can get for free. Even if they wander onto your niche site out of curiosity, they are not going there with the intent to purchase anything. They are there, above all, to enjoy that content that you're putting up and glean some sort of value from it. If you don't offer that value to them, then you are essentially providing nothing for them and they won't come back.

Keep that in mind: you aren't trying to sell them anything explicitly. You're offering them the opportunity to buy something, and if they don't take it, that's their choice.

So, with all of that in mind, let's say that you're the end user and you're looking for a site full of information about the Paleo diet. You're considering going on it, and you want to find a bunch of recipes and enough information to get started. So, you run a Google search and you see a result for "Rock Solid Eating." You think it's a clever title and you decide to check the site out.

What would you want to see, and – more importantly – what would you not want to see?

People who try to market things online make big mistakes because, too often, they sound like marketers. They don't sound lax, nor do they sound like they know what they're talking about; they just sound like guinea pigs pressing keys a thousand times trying to make a commission selling a product they don't believe in.

If you want to sell things to humans, then, believe it or not, you have to act like a human – a real human being, not somebody who types "ACT NOW!!!!!! And you'll get a FIFTY percent discount – this DEAL WON'T LAST LONG!!" trying to sell a product. While these examples are hyperbole, there genuinely are internet marketers out there who completely fail because they just don't know how to market their products. That's a shame, and you need to be smarter than to let that happen to you.

Dealing with bad reviews: It is important to understand that a part of working in the online world is taking lots of unnecessary, inaccurate, and absolutely insulting criticism. What' s more you need to realize that every product is going to get bad reviews, even those that are extremely popular. What' s more, a negative review still counts towards your overall review score so even the worst review isn't all bad. Additionally, you will likely find it heartening to know that the truly vile reviews are often ignored by users who are looking for serious flaws in your product, not pointless vitriol.

Additionally, it is important to understand that you still have the chance of salvaging the situation assuming the person actually purchased your products. If you have contact information for the negative review, the best course of action is to reach out to the customer and let them know that you are willing to work with them to ensure they are either satisfied with their purchase or satisfied with the situation. It is important to always take some time to gain perspective on the situation and never reach out to the customer when the sting of their comments is fresh in your mind.

Remember, if you can convert a bad review into a positive experience you are well on your way to creating a more positive review in the future. Other than that, if the review can be proven factually inaccurate, violates your privacy in some way or can be broadly considered obscene it can be taken down; otherwise, your best bet is to simply keep on providing quality products and quality service while also doing everything you can to ensure the positive reviews keep coming in.

Design a customer service page: You will need to interact with your customers on a regular basis. Sometimes they wish to contact you, pass a message, or make an inquiry. They need a platform to do this, and a customer service page is important.

Let them have the option of calling you, sending you a text message or even send an email message. Should you receive messages from your clients, you should respond as soon as possible. Ensure that you respond to all queries, questions, and inquiries.

Positive comments are important. So you should provide a ranking system to allow your customers to rate your products and services. This is also important and will enable you to examine your performance and hopefully improve where necessary. Always be polite to your customers no matter how hard hitting the comments. It is therefore prudent for you to act on feedback.

Finally, you should be prepared to put in the hard work every now and then. Hard work on your part means coming up with new t-shirt designs, engaging in further graphic design, marketing work such as updating your blogs and social media sites and so on.

If you work hard in the initial stages, then you can rest assured that you will enjoy a regular passive income. You will also have plenty of free time in your hands ensuring that you are free to engage in other work. This is one of the many benefits of starting a t-shirt printing business for passive income.

Add pictures to your tweets: Every time you post new content on your website you are going to want to let the world know across all your social media outlets. This should be more than a simple link, however, as studies show that if you include a picture along with a tweet then the odds of others retweeting your tweet skyrocket nearly 200 percent. Not only will this increase the eyes on your tweets, but it will also boost your overall click-through rate as well.

Don't be afraid to share content multiple times: While you may be afraid to post the same content multiple times for fear of alienating users. The fact of the matter is that based on the time of day that you do your posting, coupled with the sheer glut of content hitting social media at all times means that your target audience could very easily miss the notice regarding your latest content. To help them out, post a few times across different times of day and keep track of your results until you have honed in on the best times of day to reach the market you are aiming at.

Make yourself known: One of the most important facets of creating a meaningful connection with your target audience is creating an online persona for yourself so they don't feel as though they are simply dealing with a faceless organization. This means that you are going to want to create an "about me" page and fill it with a version of yourself that your target audience can relate to. It is important that you take the time to craft a persona that your users can relate to, even if you have to stretch the truth a little. Users will be more much likely to frequent your site if they feel as though they are connecting with a real person, even if everything else remains equal.

Focus on influencers: Especially when you are first starting out, getting your content out in front of the right sets of eyeballs is going to be just as important as creating quality content in the first place. In order to get the social media ball rolling, you may find it helpful to reach out to individuals who have a lot of pull among your target audience and send them links to the content on your site. You are going to want to do so in a way that doesn't make it look as though you are simply pandering for additional page views, but a respectful email, complete with a few links to your own work selectively thrown in, can lead to huge results assuming the influencer takes the bait and includes a link to your work across social media.

Don't make the mistake of not developing your own voice: When you are first starting to create your own unique content, it is easy to adopt a general style that is similar to the type of content you consume on a regular basis. While there is nothing inherently wrong with this approach, it is important to work to develop your own voice and style as time goes on. Remember, no matter what type of content you are producing, the internet is a big place which means that the same thing is likely being generated elsewhere in at least 1 (if not 100) different places. As such, if you are interested in creating truly unique content it is important to not focus on individual topics so much as what you can bring to the table to give the topic a unique spin.

When it comes to establishing your voice, it is perfectly acceptable to use more relaxed language, complete with plenty of slang and jargon that will show your readers that you are part of your target demographic. You are also going to want to make frequent use of the first person and talk directly to your readers to help to more fully engage them in the current conversation.

Never let quantity supersede quality: While you are going to ideally want to generate at least 3 different and unique pieces of content per week, you aren't going to ever want to sacrifice the quality of your content in order to hit that goal. Especially early on, a handful of subpar content can be enough to get new users to give up on your site entirely, a trend that can snowball if you aren't careful. As such, it is important that you always take the time to ask yourself if you would consume the content that you have created, if the answer is no then you are going to want to go back to the drawing board. If you can't hit the goal of at least 3 different pieces of quality content a week, cut back your output until the quality reaches a level you are comfortable with and then work on increasing your output from there.

Always stick to your plan: While it might seem cumbersome at first, you will find that if you get into the habit of planning out the type of content that you are creating, as well as how you plan to market it, then the process will go much more smoothly overall and you won't find yourself scrambling for new content in the middle of the week with nothing on your plate and no ideas on the horizon. Additionally, it will help to ensure that you have a constant stream of new and useful content for your target audience to consume, even if some days it is just social media based rehashes of the content you have already posted for the week. Remember, planning ahead leads to better results every single time.

Always include a call to action: Every single piece of content on your site should include not only readily available buttons that make it easy for your audience to share what they have just consumed with their friends, it should also include a personal request from you for them to share what they have just seen if they liked it and would like to do you a personal favor. While this might seem gauche, the truth of the matter is that if you don't ask for social media shares it is unlikely that you are going to get them. What's more, it is not going to turn off those who don't share as they will likely tune it out and forget that you asked as soon as they leave your page. By contrast, a personal plea can plant the idea of sharing the content in the heads of those who are agreeable to the task, even if they weren't planning on doing so in the first place.

Never let yourself run out of content: Assuming you did your homework in the proceeding chapters then it is likely that you have enough content ideas to last you a month or two when you are first getting started. During this period, it is important that you don't rest on your laurels and continue to consider new ideas wherever they may be found. One of the easiest ways to continue to find new content is to tap into the news that your target audience is going to be most interested in. Then, once you are aware of something that you feel you can work with, all you need to do is to put a personal spin on it to not only seem as though you have your finger on the pulse but to grab individuals who are looking for more details on the specific topic as well.

Additionally, keeping tabs on relevant news can easily give you ideas that are related to the topic in question while still being unique as well. Don't just focus on the most obvious facet of current news, dig deeper and consider relative topics that are on either side of the article or video you just saw. You may also have success by subscribing to as many different niche or sub-niche relevant individuals as possible as you never know when something on social media is going to catch your eye and provide you with details on a new trend that hasn't even hit the conventional news yet. The earlier you can hop on a new trend the easier it will be to capitalize on this fact and generate a significant bump in page views as a result.

Don't be afraid to repurpose content from time to time: Just because you have covered a specific topic once, doesn't mean that you can' revisit it again in the future or even repurpose a majority of it for a second run in a different format. For example, if you create a blog post about a relevant issue, then a few months later you can generate a video, or series of videos, utilizing the same basic topic while still generating a significant amount of extra viewers while doing only a small amount of new work depending on the quality of the video as well as its scope.

Outside of turning blog posts into videos, you can also turn a series of blog posts into an eBook with very little additional effort as long as one blog naturally flows into the next. What's more, you can then sell the book to make an extra profit or, even better, give the book away for free in exchange for a site signup or something similar. Giving away something free is always going to be a huge draw on any website, especially if the content is fairly above par, to begin with. In fact, if you start to make it a habit of repurposing your content you will find it much easier to do so if you keep in mind how you are going to repurpose it in the initial content creation stage.

Bring followers into the conversation: Once you have developed a reliable following among your target audience, it is important to consider them as a reliable resource when it comes to generating new content ideas. Not only will particularly dedicated members of your community often pitch you ideas that will make great content, but they may also have personal stories that will do the job just as well. Don't be afraid to reach out to your target audience and ask to hear their stories. Not only will this lead to great content on its own, but it will also show them that you care about what they think and lead to a greater sense of connection as well.

Start a consistent posting strategy: Posting on Instagram can be tricky. There are a lot of variables that you have to consider. You have to decide what times you want to post at. You have to decide what content you want to post on the page. And you have to decide how many times you would like to post on the page. Each company is going to have a different posting strategy that works for them. But the number one thing that you can concentrate on when it comes to this is coming up with a posting strategy that is consistent.

Consistency is key no matter which social media platform you decide to work with. You are never going to see results if you can't post your content on a regular basis. If you post a bunch for a month, and then go with just one posting a week, and then back to two posts a day, and then you go silent for three months, and so on, you will find that it is really hard to maintain the following that you want on the profile.

Your followers want to feel that there is some consistency to your posting. They don't want to feel like you are just using them to make money and then disappearing once they purchase from you, or once you get bored with the whole thing. Figure out what kind of schedule not only gets the best response from your followers, but also works the best for you, and then stick with that. Over the long term, this will give you the best results.

Chapter 10: Social Media Myths

Instagram is irrelevant: The first myth commonly told by marketing gurus is that Instagram does not matter and that you can easily grow your business anywhere else without the use of Instagram. The reality is that Instagram is actually one of the largest social media platforms out there and virtually every single company can increase their audience and conversion ratio through Instagram if they use it properly.

There are no specific models that work best on Instagram, as every company can get on Instagram and start creating a unique strategy that works best for them. If you have a company in the 21st century, you need to be building your audience on Instagram. Even if your audience consists primarily of seniors or children, or people who would likely not be on Instagram, the people who will be supporting these individuals in purchasing things will be on Instagram.

Email marketing is dead: While some people may consider email marketing a fad whose time has come and gone; the truth of the matter is that it is still an extreme marketing force to be reckoned with but only when it is done properly. Ideally, you will be gathering followers via your campaign to become an authority, while also sending emails to your customers to help improve the likelihood of your products receiving the types of verified reviews you are looking for.

In your blog posts and on your social media pages you are going to want to put out a call to your followers and let them know that you are going to be starting an email newsletter and then let them know where they send their details to sign up. Additionally, you can add a subscription link to your customer emails and offer them your book free of charge if they sign up. Even if they don't sign up, the promise of something with perceived value is enough to ensure the solicitation isn't seen as an issue. Even if you otherwise have access to customer email addresses, it is important to never send email without permission as all it takes is a single instance of someone hitting the spam button to negate any chance of ever reaching them again.

When it comes to generating the right type of content, you are going to want to segment your customer email base by their demographics to ensure you put out the right targeted content for each market. Luckily, you will be able to have a clear idea of their past search histories based on the information that Amazon provides which should make it easy to determine the general demographics and if they differ from your target audience.

When it comes to generating content for your newsletter you are going to want to include a mix of niche related content as well as advertising and weekly deals. Your goal should always be to provide valuable content in addition to advertising as it will keep more of your customer base coming back over longer periods of time. Likewise, it is important to ensure that the email newsletter showcases your humanity as someone your target audience can relate to as the face of your brand. This means you are going to want to look like your target audience would expect in the picture you include with each email personal greeting. You will also want to include anecdotes about your life and niche specific activities to show you are more than just an authority or an expert, you, and your target audience are kindred spirits.

How and when you send out your emails is just as important as the content you include as if you can't catch the attention of your audience in that first instant, then it won't matter how insightful or useful your email newsletter is. The first thing you need to do is consider the subject line that you use for your email newsletters, and whatever you do, avoid subject lines that are between 60 and 70 characters. Longer subject lines are fine and shorter are more effective but for some reason, marketers can't quite agree on, 60 to 70 characters is a death knell when it comes to your email open rate.

The time of day and the day of the week are also important considerations to factor into your email marketing plans. Studies show that you are more likely to see success in terms of both open rate and click-throughs to your products if you send your email newsletter either late at night or on the weekends. The idea here is that if you manage to catch your target audience when they are less worried about the hustle and bustle of the day you have a greater chance of drawing them in and generating a conversion in the process.

When composing an email newsletter, it is important to always do so with an eye towards mobile interactions. This means you will want to stick to single column content and use a font that is a bit larger than might otherwise seem a natural choice. You will also want to ensure you can enable touch-based interactions including buttons that are 44x44 pixels.

It is important to choose an email marketing platform that will allow you the freedom to generate the types of emails you choose on the schedule that works for you. MailChimp offers a free starter service that is a great way to get started in the space while at the same time providing you with plenty of room to grow as the needs of your email marketing campaign change. It will also make it easy for you to segment customers in various beneficial ways while at the same time making it simple to send out follow up emails in which you can offer surveys whose results can help you gather additional data which will, in turn, help you make your email newsletters more effective.

Social media is only for creating new customers: If you have ever heard that social media is specifically meant for gaining new customers, then you have heard another common myth in the social media marketing world. The truth is: social media is not exclusively for creating new customers, it is also for retaining customers. In fact, a recent study showed that 84% of most brands on Facebook are being followed by people who were customers first and who went on to find them on social media, not by new customers who have never shopped with the brand at all. This statistic likely varies across all of the different platforms, but the fact remains that social media is a powerful tool for staying in touch with your existing audience and maintaining their loyalty. When you encourage your existing customers to follow you, you create the opportunity to maintain and grow your relationship with them, which supports you in bringing existing customers back and turning them into loyal fans of your brand.

Video content does not matter: Many people feel intimidated by the creation of video content and, unfortunately, are being told by mediocre marketing strategists that they can effectively use the platform without video marketing. The truth is: you can use the platform and create success without videos, but you are not going to create nearly as much as you could if you were to incorporate video content into your strategy. At the end of the day, your followers want to feel connected with your brand and with the people who are running the brand, which is done best by creating video content for your followers to engage with.

You can create video content through your stories, live videos, IGTV, or even creating short videos to use as posts or as display ads.

When you are creating videos, make sure that you create high-quality videos and that you focus on getting yourself comfortable on camera. Since video marketing is growing in popularity, there are many people using high-quality equipment, professional lighting, and who are great on camera. While you do not need to have professional equipment or be a daytime television star, using a high-quality light or sitting in natural light, using a camera that shoots in at least 1080p (most new smartphones shoot in 1080p or 4k), and by practicing frequently. The more you practice shooting videos, the more you are going to feel confident in creating them and the better your videos are going to get over time. As you grow larger, you can also consider having a professional videographer working together with you to create professional videos for your advertisements and posts. Again, this is not necessary, but you can certainly do it if you want to step up your game and have higher quality content.

Any content is good content: People shouldn't ever feel like they're wasting their time and resources by following your account. The content you post should always do something that either peaks their interest, engages with them, or promotes something.

Users are also more likely to feel like they are getting something out of following your company on social media if you post content that they will find useful or informative. This method is especially effective if you are in an industry associated with technology, craftsmanship, or any other industry that has customers that are knowledgeable or creative.

You can do this by posting images such as infographics or guides. You can also turn your audience onto free tools, extensions, or other interesting, helpful things. If your platform allows it, you could also post educational or specialized videos that will appeal to your audience.

Creating a membership club among your customers that offers discounts and ensures many of them keep coming back. Other perks you could offer your audience include free shipping, bulk deals, and general coupons. Not only will this keep your customers actively following you on social media, but it also encourages customer loyalty and has the potential to entice new customers should they stumble onto your page.

Stories are a passing fad: Creating stories on Instagram is a great way to get organic reach and it does not require large quantities of equipment. By using stories, you are doing a similar action that would be taken on Facebook stories. They will appear above your image feed on your page and when people log in to their Instagram it appears at the top of their followers feed.

You can use these to draw some attention to your content and build some engaged in interactive communication. The same as Facebook stories, Instagram stories are highly informal but a great way to post content to your Instagram feed so that others can see your day to day. It is also a great way to provide insight into your new product lines or create excitement for a coming product that is a surprise. Instagram stories provide a seamless way to create continuously content that keeps your page relevant and up to date. You can use your Instagram story to provide a daily message to your fans without the overwhelming content and communication that would come from posting every hour or so. One of the good things that Instagram stories provide you with is a seamless and affordable way to produce videos without concern for quality. During your stories, you can create a CTA that will help you gain more clients as well as, build engagement. Since Instagram stories are known to receive more views than any other post, this is the most important way to engage with your consumers.

Social is not measurable: Social is extremely measurable, but first, you have to do something that can be measured. Tracking URLs, visibility into your purchase funnel, unified customer databases. All of it can answer that "are we making money at this?" question, but too often people expect there to be a magic "social media measurement" button, even though there is no such button for radio, TV, email, direct mail, billboards, or fancy business cards.

While you may have to look for the metrics a little more, they are most definitely there, regardless of which platform you choose to use. In addition to the tools available from each of the major social media platforms, it is important to do ancillary research and see what third-party options are out there for tracking metrics for the social media platforms you are placing the highest overall priority on. There is literally no such thing as too much information on your target audience so the more ways you can discover to track it, the better.

Tracking the data is only half the battle, of course, it is then equally important that you use that information in the most effective way possible. This means carefully tracking the content you generate in order to determine what offerings appeal to what segments of your target audience as a means of separating those that underperform from those whose ROI is off the charts. As long as you make an effort to vary your content early on and meticulously categorize it in your notes, there is no reason you should be able to know exactly how effective each piece of content is going to be, and who will likely be clicking on it before a single view has been recorded.

Conclusion

Thanks for making it through to the end of *Social Media Marketing 2019: The Power Of Instagram Marketing - How to Win Followers & Influence Millions Online Using Highly Effective Personal Branding & Digital Networking Strategies,* let's hope it was informative and able to provide you with all of the tools you need to achieve your goals. Just because you've finished this book doesn't mean there is nothing left to learn on the topic, and expanding your horizons is the only way to find the mastery you seek.

Now that you have made it to the end of this book, you hopefully have an understanding of how to get started using Instagram for social media marketing, as well as a strategy or two, or three, that you are anxious to try for the first time. Before you go ahead and start giving it your all, it is important that you have realistic expectations as to the level of success you should expect in the near future.

While it is perfectly true that some people experience serious success right out of the gate, it is an unfortunate fact of life that they are the exception rather than the rule. What this means is that you should expect to experience something of a learning curve, especially when you are first figuring out what works for you. This is perfectly normal, however, and if you persevere you will come out the other side better because of it. Instead of getting your hopes up to an unrealistic degree, you should think of your time spent growing your brand on Instagram as a marathon rather than a sprint which means that slow and steady will win the race every single time.

Finally, if you found this book useful in any way, a review on Amazon is always appreciated!

Social Media Marketing 2019

How to Brand Yourself Online Through Facebook, Twitter, YouTube & Instagram - Highly Effective Strategies for Digital Networking, Personal Branding, and Online Influence

Robert Miller

Table of Contents

Introduction

Congratulations on getting a copy of *Social Media Marketing 2019: How to Brand Yourself Online Through Facebook, Twitter, YouTube & Instagram - Highly Effective Strategies for Digital Networking, Personal Branding, and Online Influence.* With so many options available in every niche, finding ways to make your business stand out can be difficult, especially for those just starting out. This is what makes branding so important as it is what will help turn your brand from one of the pack—to one of a kind.

The best way to make your brand stand out these days is through social media and the following chapters will discuss everything you need to do in order to get started successfully. First, you will learn the basics of branding and the things you need to consider before getting started to ensure the best results. Next, you will learn about the new trends that are going to shape 2019 from start to finish.

With the basics out of the way, you will then learn about the things to keep in mind when creating your brand to ensure that you stand out from the crowd. You will also find chapters dedicated to helping your personality shine through in your work and ways to find your audience. You will then learn how to create an offer that is irresistible as well as find tips for staying on brand regardless if you are using Facebook, Instagram or YouTube. Finally, you will find tips for finding and keeping a mentor that is worth the trouble and how to keep tabs on your brand once things are running smoothly.

There are plenty of books on this subject on the market, thanks again for choosing this one! Every effort was made to ensure it is full of as much useful information as possible, please enjoy!

Chapter 1: Branding Basics

Branding is the process of creating a mental resonance between you and your image. It is comprised of a symbol, a design, a name, a sound, a reputation, a series of emotions, employees, your tone, and so much more. The entire package, known as a branding package, is specifically designed to create a "character" for your company. Branding, then, is building a relationship between that "character" and your audience.

For as long as one person has needed to convince another of the superiority of one object over another virtually identical object, the brand has been an essential element of a successful business. Companies designed brands as a way to make their name memorable, tangible, and identifiable. The idea was that if your brand could easily be identified, your audience would remember you and would be more likely to purchase from you. It is likely that this was just a basic idea in the beginning, but branding has gone on to represent a powerful psychological reaction, as it has been refined over the years.

This psychological reaction that causes you to recall a brand, even if it was not triggered by something that brand put out for you to see, is something that branding relies on. It is the same as remembering a close friend every time you see frogs because you know they like frogs, or remembering a specific memory with your mother every time you make a turkey at Thanksgiving because that was a fond memory the two of you shared. The psychological reaction, then, is the same as you having a relationship with the brand. It is powerful, it is emotionally charged, and it creates a deep attachment that carries some sort of meaning for you.

Branding is not just an age-old practice that businesses continue to use just because it is commonplace. Now more than ever, branding is essential, as there are more choices out there for your potential customers than ever before. Your personal brand is more than a logo or a style guide for marketing efforts. It can be thought of as everything that differentiates your social media presence from the competition as a good brand influences every aspect of your customer's experience. A good brand can generate significant additional awareness while a bad one can ruin you regardless of the quality of whatever it is you ultimately produce.

The goal of every business is to be the first choice for their target audience, bar none and managing and building a brand is a major step in making that happen. While the first thing that most people think of when it comes to branding are the things that were listed off at the start of this chapter, the concept of the brand actually extends beyond that to things like the core values of your business and even peaks through in every interaction you have with suppliers and customers so much so that it reflects the reputation of your organization.

It isn't just customers that build up an emotional attachment to specific brands either, employees of certain companies are well known for being overly committed to their corporate overlords making it possible for strong loyalties to rise to the point that they even come with a sense of ownership as well. This can be an effective tool when it comes to increasing sales, as well as maintaining employee motivation. It can also cause problems as your company grows, however, if those who feel they are stakeholders do not feel they were properly consulted when it came to planning out the future of the company.

In this day and age products or services that are truly unique are practically non-existent which means what you are only ever really selling your customers is your brand which is why it is important that yours is strong enough to stand out. Successful branding is all about promoting your strengths which is why you want to start by thinking about what sets your business apart from the pack. Good places to start include things like:

- Skills that make your business uniquely qualified
- Outstanding customer service
- Better than the average value
- Unique innovation

Understanding what customers want

It is important to ensure that whatever your company's promise, you always deliver based on your existing strengths and brand values which make up the basis of the assumptions your customers have when they first encounter your business. If the customers' requirements and your brand values aren't in perfect alignment then there will be issues with their expectations and your performance that can't be resolved easily.

In order to ensure these things align properly, you will first want to consider the primary motivations of your customers and the things that trigger them to make a purchase in your niche. While performance and price are going to be near the top of the list, there is often more to the story when it comes to customer motivation.

A great place to start when it comes to determining that missing extra something is by asking your existing customers what they feel your brand's greatest strengths are. From there, you will want to speak with potential future customers in your niche and ask what they look for prior to making a decision to buy. This will allow you to match your perceived strengths with niche demands to ensure your brand delivers on expectations from both fronts.

If your values are already properly aligned then you are ready to start building on the strong foundations of your future brand. However, if things aren't properly aligned then the first thing you are going to need to do is to reconsider the benefits you are showing the customer upfront, as well as if you are currently focusing on the proper target audience.

As an example, if you own a high fashion clothing store then your brand value can be increased by focusing on the fact that your target audience is only interested in the trendiest, priciest products. If they instead tried to focus their efforts by trying for mass appeal, they would only be wasting money by not focusing on the needs of their target audience.

In order to ensure you are proceeding on the right foot, it is recommended that you sit down and take some time to generate a document that outlines what your brand's core values are as well as benchmarks to show those values are enforced and expressed to the target audience. The goal for your core value should be to encapsulate the entire purpose of your business and what separates you from the competition.

Building your brand: In order to maintain and build a strong brand, it is important to focus on exactly what your customers want so that you can determine the most effective way that you can ultimately deliver it. You will want to be consistent with your service as well as at any other point where your customers come into direct contact with you.

After you have considered the needs of your customers as well as your brand values, you will be able to start consistently building your brand by regularly communicating your brand values. When doing so it is important to keep in mind that each and every contact you have with a customer or potential customer needs to actively reinforce your brand values in a meaningful way. While you don't want to beat your customer's over the head with how great your brand is, there are a few key areas you should focus on including:

- your business name
- the names of your products or services
- any slogan you use
- your logo
- the style and quality of your stationery
- product pricing and packaging
- your premises
- where and how you advertise
- how you and your employees dress
- how you and your employees behave
- your company website

If each of the above can be said to remain consistently in line with your existing brand values then you can expect overall brand growth in the long-term. If they are not all in line, however, then your business and your brand could be seriously damaged, possibly beyond repair. Your brand presence can be thought of as a promise that you make to your customers and if it isn't kept then you can bet that your first-time customers are going to be far less likely to come back a second time. Generally speaking, the only things that a customer will remember are the best thing about their experience with your brand and the worst thing; it is your job to ensure the former outshines the latter.

For these reasons, it is also very important to treat the use of your logo with care. You should have a clear policy on when it can be used and what it can be placed on to ensure that a consistent level of quality is always maintained. Your logo should be akin to a seal of quality that reassures your customer's that they made the right choice and if this is not the case then you need to consider what can be done about it as quickly as possible.

Similarly, ensure that you consider the design and quality of your invoices and receipts, which can often be the last stage in an interaction with a customer. This can affect their willingness to give you repeat custom and even to pay on time.

Manage your brand: When it comes to keeping up with brand strategy in the long-term, it is important that there is one guiding hand at the helm to ensure that everything feels cohesive. While one person should ultimately be in charge, everyone who is a part of your team is going to be involved in maintaining the brand as the way they act towards customers will impact what those customers think about your business. If your team believes in what your brand stands for then their actions will indicate as much, providing effective evidence that your brand stands up for what it believes in.

In order to ensure that team members are properly towing the line, it is important to regularly take the time to discuss with them concerns they might have about the brand and overall how well the brand's stated goals are being met. It is important to make the message that the brand represents part of the corporate culture of the company, not just as lip service but in such a way, that every member of the team understands why approaching things in a specific way is the best choice for everyone involved. Likewise, it is important that everyone understands that creating a negative experience for even one customer, even once, is enough to potentially damage the brand in a serious way.

Externally, it is important to ensure that your brand is on track by regularly reaching out to existing customers for honest feedback. It is important to reach out to customers that did not return for a second visit or those that reached out with negative comments for their input. This is often one of the best ways to see the type of feedback that will help you reach new audiences in the future.

It is important to take the time to reach out to your customers on a regular basis so you can keep an eye on changing trends as well. Doing so will make it possible for your company to change with your target audience and ensure you remain relevant in the long-term. It doesn't matter how well-established your brand is, you will always need to maintain a strict focus on relevancy in order to remain on top.

Review your brand: Once you reach a point where your brand is successful, you can count on remaining so as long as you maintain your existing values and remain relevant to your customers which is why it is important to review your brand regularly, even if you are not yet at the top of your game. When reviewing your brand, even if you are only cutting what appears to be dead weight, it is important to keep in mind that existing team members and customers alike may feel connected to that which you are taking away. As such, when you come across things that appear to be negatives, it is important to consider them from all angles before you end up accidentally making a change you will need to take back at a later date.

What you should avoid doing at any cost is making the mistake of simply running away from your problems by rebranding yourself and trying again. Not only is this process very expensive, but the internet also has a long memory and it doesn't like those who try to lie to it. Unless you move your operations to a new country and start from scratch then not only will this strategy not work, it will sour the goodwill of those who were still on your side because no one likes someone who tries to run away from their problems. Instead of hiding from your problems, it is always going to be easier to fix the underlying issues and work to rebuild customer trust naturally.

Don't forget, your brand represents the entirety of the customer experience, not just the color scheme of your website or your logo; it represents the sum total of the customer's experience which is why it can't be changed overnight. This is why it is important to regularly review your customers' experience so you can catch any problems while they are still gestating to prevent an issue that is large enough that your brand won't be able to come back from it.

Budget for your brand: Due to the fact that your brand is going to include a variety of areas from your business, it can be difficult to create an accurate budget, and to maintain an existing budget as well. Regardless, you are still going to want to limit things as much as you can to avoid spending money and getting nothing in return. A budget will also help you to focus on those things that are the most important in the short-term so you can prioritize effectively. Important resources to budget for early on include:

- design needs, such as a logo, signage, business stationery or product packaging
- your premises

234

- your advertising
- time you'll need to spend with employees to make sure they understand your brand
- any resources you'll have to provide for employees to enable them to carry out what the brand promises, e.g. customer service costs
- keeping your company website updated

Don't forget, you don't need to do everything at once, as long as your team understands what their deliverables are and what the promises of your brand are, you are getting started on the right track.

Chapter 2: What's New in 2019

New forms of engagement, challenges, and formats make 2019 an exciting time to be a brand on social media.

Increased need for trust: The first new trend of 2019 will focus on bringing out the human angle of a given brand even more as the circle of trust on social media constricts even more. This can be seen across a variety of social media platforms, starting with Facebook taking steps to improve accuracy, transparency, and security in the wake of a congressional hearing and the Cambridge Analytica scandal. During this same timeframe, Twitter has been fighting off its own controversies over an increasing number of bots on its service by purging millions of fake accounts.

During this period of time regulators and consumers alike have questioned the ethics, accuracy, and privacy of every major social network. The end result of this social media witch hunt is that a record 60 percent of users no longer trust brand messages that come via social media. Unsurprisingly, this presents new challenges for brands as users stop listening to celebrity influencers and instead start listening to micro-influencers in record droves. Outside of these stalwarts who are respected for being real people, trust has largely reverted back to pre-social media sources including family, friends, personal acquaintances and trusted news outlets.

This had already lead smart brands to begin focusing less on overall reach and more on generating quality engagement that appears transparent from the start. The goal should now be to work on developing smaller, more intimate target audience groups so that a meaningful dialog can develop on its own. The focus should be on creating communities and letting those in the communities talk to one another as opposed to inundating the group with sales-based messages that are more likely to simply be ignored.

A great way to get started down this path is to create a branded Instagram hashtag that is aligned with key community values. In order to build an effective conversation around your brand, you will need to create a short, hashtag that is branded and easy to remember so that it can serve as a linchpin that will bring the community together around common interests. A good example of this is the Herschel Supply Co which uses the well-traveled hashtag to encourage its target audience to send in their pictures of Herschel merchandise being used all around the world. You can use your own hashtags to help properly align users with your brand's values as opposed to just showing off new products.

Another great choice is to run a Twitter chat which is a public discussion on Twitter about a specific hashtag. This is a great way to get your community engaged with one another by creating lively discussions based on shared target audience interests. These chats are held in real-time, and the flow of the conversation is led by you, the moderator.

The key here is for brands to create a space where customers can freely congregate and talk to one another which is why you want to spark the engagement and then let the community influence and police itself. The last thing you want to do when you have created this type of space is to destroy the goodwill you have created by filling it with product plugs and obvious sales pitches. This group can be public or private though it should be well-promoted so everyone is clear on why it exists.

Once you have a basic space created for this purpose, you can then move on to looking into micro-influencers in your space to further improve upon the quality of your reach within your target audience. This is an especially effective approach with smaller niches where even the micro-influencers are well known by almost everyone. These individuals are likely already going to have the type of extremely engaged social media presence that you are looking for. They are going to be far more cost-effective than celebrity influencers as well, despite being viewed as the most trustworthy and thus likely to have the highest percentage of conversions based on follower size. You can track down relevant micro-influencers with a quick hashtag search on Instagram or Twitter.

Another great choice is to start a secret Facebook group, which is a group that is not open to everyone and cannot be found with a simple Facebook search. The only way new members can join this type of group is if an existing member invites them. While not the right choice for every brand, for those that prioritize exclusivity, this is a great way to take things to the next level. What' s more, knowing that the group is private tends to convince most people to share more freely as they feel closer to the other people in the group by default.

Stories, stories, stories: Story shares are growing at a rate that is 15-times faster than traditional feed-based shares. In fact, Facebook's CPO recently shared a chart showing that stories are set to surpass feeds as the primary means of sharing by 2020. As there are already nearly a billion users with access to stories across WhatsApp, Snapchat, Facebook and Instagram, this prediction doesn't seem that far off.

While this is not surprising when one looks at the number of stories prominently displayed across all types of social media, what is surprising is what this change is indicative of which is that social media is finally going to be focused on mobile first. With Facebook as the social media touchstone that people of all ages can relate to, the end focus was still designed for laptop and desktop computer use. The truly mobile-only always online networks designed for today allow users to capture in-the-moment experiences like never before and stories are leading the charge.

Stories are overwhelmingly visual and meant to be created and consumed on the fly with nothing more than a smartphone and a creative eye. What's more, as they only last for a limited period of time it is more likely that users will have fun and take risks with their photos than with those they know may be available permanently on other social media sites. This has the side effect of making stories feel more personal, immediate and all around real than other types of social media.

While it shouldn't be hard for brands to understand why this type of approach is useful, it will require a shift of focus for 2019 to make the goal a reality. While there will always be value in high-value posts, taking the time to create stories that are less tightly edited, not more, will become more and more important which means balancing differing content styles is going to become more important as well. Brands have to accept the fact that highly curated content isn't always best. The new generation prefers authentic content, and they are experts at sniffing out inauthenticity.

Preparing to capitalize on this trend is as easy as starting to experiment with stories. Nearly four out of five major brands are already on the story bandwagon which means if you don't start soon you will miss out. Luckily, creating stories is easier and there is a low barrier to entry, as long as you record your videos vertically (once the ultimate indicator of a lack of technical proficiency) then you are good to go. Make sure you experiment with posting your stories at different times of day and throughout the week to see what your followers respond best to.

Once you are familiar with the basics of stories, the next thing you are going to want to focus on is creating content that is story specific. The content you create for your stories needs to reflect the unique look and feel that those who consume stories have already come to expect. This includes live, unedited action that is completely devoid of editorial style or filters. These types of stories will perform better because they use the aesthetic your followers have already been conditioned to want to see.

As your stories will likely require a fair amount of time and effort to create, especially if they look spontaneous and simple, it is only natural that you wouldn't want them to disappear after just 24 hours. This is where the Highlights feature comes into play as it allows you to display specific stories for as long as you like. Choosing this option will display the chosen stories along with your cover image. This is a great way to highlight things like campaigns, special promotions or other, longer, videos that deserve some time in the spotlight.

It is important to show some restraint when highlighting stories, however, as people like stories precisely because they are ephemeral. If you highlight a few stories and then stop making new ones people will just become bored with your content and stop visiting your page regularly.

Once you have spent some time perfecting your story technique, you can take things to the next level and mix things up when it comes to the structures of your stories as a means of finding new ways to show off your brand. This could take the form of things like a question and answer session about a topic you know your target audience might like, a behind the scenes look at your company or a tutorial on how to use your product in a way that maximizes your value.

Determining what is the most successful is done by adding UTMs to your links. If your business account reaches 10,000 followers it will allow you to add a feature to your stories that allows users to swipe up to go to your landing page or website. Accessing this feature will show you just how effective each of your stories is for your brand because you will see the effects in the web traffic your stories generate.

While stories are already old hat on some forms of social media, one area where there is still room to get in on the ground floor is with Facebook stories. At the end of 2018, only about 10 percent of brands were using stories on Facebook which means that slightly repurposing your content could lead to a serious increase in conversions. What's more, it is extremely easy to do, as there is a button that allows you to syndicate stories between Instagram and Facebook.

The current bleeding edge of stories lies in custom GIFs and AR which both allow the storytelling to advance to a whole new level. Both are now available features on modern smartphone cameras and GIFs can be used to grab extra attention and place even more focus on a specific call to action.

Close the ad gap: The pay-to-play era of social media has been going on for more than a decade and social media brand spending was up 32 percent in 2018. In fact, 25 percent of all Facebook pages now use some type of paid media with

Facebook as a whole accounting for nearly 25 percent of all digital ad spending. However, the rising costs don't always align with increased attention from followers. Instead, this increased spending needs to come with increasing investment in creativity and marketing savvy with paid boosts going to increase organic content.

Brands of all sizes are building out their social teams in droves with skilled cross-platform content creators versed in video, motion graphics, design, and more. Enhanced third-party ad targeting tools, which enable easy A/B testing (in some cases with hundreds of variants), are also becoming the norm.

Social networks all have different targeting options depending on the type of ad you are looking to create and an increased focus on the differences between them will be rewarded with increased follower conversion in the future. It will also make it easier to determine how they interact with your services, products, business, and brand as a whole.

When determining how much focus to put towards this arena it is important to have clear metrics and goals that show the bottom-line impact social media has on your business. The metrics that matter most to you are going to depending on the type of campaign you are running as well as the goals you have and the audience you are interested in reaching. For example, if the goal of your campaign is to raise awareness, then you might be more interested in impressions while if your goal was to increase conversion you would place more emphasis on increasing click-throughs.

With brands paying big bucks to compete for follower attention on social media, it is no longer acceptable to just create content, the things you need to create must resonate with your audience. This means things like compelling visuals, interesting stories, and useful tips if you want to see more than just clicks and hope to actually increase conversions. Not every brand is going to have the capital to hire a professional film crew, but even splurging a little bit to hire a freelancer can make a great difference.

A great place to start is by repurposing concepts that have already proven successful with your target audience in other places. Creating social ads that promote your brand properly takes time and money which makes it far more economical to test out a concept you are brainstorming with a post on your website before moving forward. Once you know what's working you will be able to repurpose and adapt as needed, confident that your hard work will be worth it in the end.

Chapter 3: Creating Your Brand

During the early days, you are likely going to always feel strapped for resources. As such, it is important to focus first on creating a brand, as it will ultimately influence almost every other facet of your operation. These days a good brand is the sum total of the way your social media presence looks and feels and also determines who it speaks too and thus who your follower base is going to be. Regardless of the type of social media account you are planning on starting, your brand identity should be given serious thought. While the specifics of what constitutes brand identity can be a bit vague, for the purposes of the remainder of this chapter you can assume it includes graphics and visual presentation, design, iconography, typography, color palette and logo. There are certainly other elements you can include in this list, but these should be enough to get you moving in the right direction.

Think hard about your target audience: When it comes to building a brand, the first thing you are going to want to do is to determine who your target audience is going to be. This is largely going to be influenced by the niche you've chosen, as well as the items that you have your eye on selling. When determining who your target audience is going to be, you are going to want to start by taking to social media and seeing what sorts of people are talking about the products you are thinking about selling.

It is important to really do your research during this step as you want to identify as many interconnected characteristics that you can target amongst those most likely to buy your products for the best results. If you are already a part of this group, then even better, if not, once you have a clear idea of who you are targeting, you are going to want to find out everything about them. This means the types of products they enjoy and what their buying habits are, but also what type of design tends to appeal to their demographic and what their thoughts and values are more likely to be.

If your target audience is under the age of 40, a good way to do this is to go to YouTube and see what type of content is being produced that is related to your target niche. This will give you a good idea of what type of tone is likely to appeal to your target audience and also what type of phrasing and slang to use in your branding.

Choosing a name

While it doesn't take much to pick out a bad username when you see it, understanding what it takes to create a good name can be much more complicated. To get started, you may want to consider which of the three primary name conventions, whimsical, evocative or descriptive, that you want to explore more fully. Descriptive names are self-explanatory, much like the names themselves and include what the primary focus of the account will be. Alternately you can go with something that is evocative without really being descriptive which will prevent you from having to stick to a narrowly defined topic.

Know what's popular: When it comes to creating a useful username, it will automatically make it easier for you to attract new followers if people can find you by simply searching for your primary niche. The best way to go about picking out the optimal search terms for your niche is to utilize a website like UberSuggest.org. All you need to do is enter any word into its search bar and it will provide you with all of the most popular search terms related to it.

Consider related words: If you don't have anything catchy in mind right off the bat, the first thing you are going to want to consider is words that are naturally related to your niche while also reflecting your unique take on it. A thesaurus of either the physical or digital sort is a great place to start and you never know when a new word might spark the creative notion that gives birth to your new business name. If nothing jumps out at you right from the start, simply make a list of between 50 and 100 potential options and save them for later.

Cast a wide net: Once you have a decent list of words at your disposal, you are going to want to start playing around with them in such a way that they start generating some ideas. A good place to start is with names based around puns. Regardless of how you feel about puns personally, they are a great starting off point and will serve to get your brain in the right type of name creating mindset. Pungenerator.org is a great place to start, just be aware that you may need to put in some time before anything worthwhile surfaces.

Don't end up in a hurry to choose something: If you end up spending an undue amount of time trying to come up with the right name, it can be easy to lose focus and wander off onto a path of logic that no user is going to be able to follow you down. This is why it is important to test the name with other people for a few days to ensure that they pick up what you are laying down. Talk about the name with your friends and family, text it, email it, write it down, try it with different fonts and different sizes to see what you think about it from as many angles as possible. If things work out, then great; otherwise, you will need to be ready to go back to the drawing board and start from scratch.

Create a logo

When it comes to creating a successful logo, the first thing you will need to keep in mind is just how omnipresent that it is going to be. In addition to being on all of your products, it is going to be on all of your email correspondence as well as on any advertising that you might want to pay for down the line. This means that the most important consideration of all is always going to be picking something that is malleable enough to expand or contract as needed. After that, consider the colors and fonts that will speak to your target audience most directly.

A perfect logo is one that can be immediately linked to a specific brand, and the company that sells it. When it is created with the right amount of care, a good logo can represent the values and mission statement of your business as well, all with just a single look. If a picture is worth a thousand words, a good logo is worth a thousand conversions, but only if it is done properly. In many cases, a great place to start is a common symbol that potential customers are likely to encounter in their daily interactions as well as on your labels.

If your marketing is successful then your target audience will think of your brand whenever that symbol presents itself, essentially hijacking any other purpose that symbol might have. If you don't think that is likely, consider #. Did you think of that as the phrase "pound key" or did you simply see a hashtag? Twitter took # and if you claim a symbol of your own your target audience won't be able to get away from your brand even if you try.

Additionally, you are going to want a logo that is bold as well as vibrant in such a way that it is sure to catch the eye of any potential customers when they see it as part of your marketing campaign. It also needs to be both clear and visually simple enough for potential customers to instantly have an idea of what they are looking at so they can absorb your branding instead of scratching their heads over just what it is they are looking at.

Consider your message: The first thing you will want to take some time to think about is the message that you want your logo to clearly convey. This is going to be something fairly straightforward as anything complicated is likely to get lost in the shuffle. If you are having trouble, consider the reason that you wanted to start your website in the first place and then think about the ways that you can sum up your goal in a single sentence. Keep this single sentence handy and refer to it from time to time to ensure everything is staying on message.

Beyond determining what you want to communicate about your brand, you will also need to consider the tone you will want to present as well. This decision shouldn't be made in a vacuum, it should be based on your goals for your site as well as what other people in your niche are currently up to as well.

Develop a mission statement

When combined with a value proposition, a quality mission statement will ensure you leave a good first impression on visitors to your site about your contributions to the world at large. The following guidelines will help you craft a quality mission statement.

Aim big: Good mission statements should be about something bigger than yourself that should ideally connect you and your potential customers together in an emotional way. The thing you choose should matter in the big picture, it also helps if it is something your company actually does.

Be the best: The mission statement you create should be one that makes it clear you are striving to do more than simply be the best at what you do. This type of statement is inward focused when instead it needs to be outward facing and put the customer first.

Focus on what's tangible: The best mission statements don't make grand claims, they focus on the connection that customers have to the business based on their products or services, creating a tangible link that the customer can hold onto as a promise of future growth.

Be yourself: Your mission statement should be as unique as your company. It should express what you do in a clear way that goes beyond just listing the facts. Your mission statement should reflect your brand and everything that makes what you offer so wonderful and unique.

Putting it all together: While creating value is crucial to growing your business in the long-term, making it clear what it is you do exactly is crucial when it comes to getting customers to choose you over your competition. Once you have successfully created your value statement it is important to look at it from every angle and ensure it is as focused on the customer as possible. If you find that what you created talks more about the company than the clients then you are going to want to go back to the drawing board and try again. To ensure you get it right, make it a point of reading it as if you were someone who had never visited your site before today.

Additional social media considerations

Branding successfully on social media is an achievable goal. To get the most out of the social media platforms, a company needs to:

- *Develop a strong voice:* Your brand's personality and voice should reflect in every message and post that is being put on the business social media page. Be authentic, be genuine and be true to your brand. Do not fall into the trap of trying to copying another brand's voice and style of presenting itself on social media. What works for one brand may not work for your brand. Find your own voice, find your own style, and be consistent in the way that voice is delivered to your audience so they will come to associate it with your brand.

- *Connect with the audience:* Speak to them as if they matter. Because they do. They are the heart and soul of any business and without an audience, there would be no business. Speak to them and connect with them on their terms, and develop brand messages and posts that they can relate with to strengthen your brand.

- *Post useful content:* Posting multiple times a day with frivolous information that does nothing to strengthen your brand image is just going to be a waste of time. Content needs to be original, useful and engaging.

- *Engage, engage, engage:* Always engage with your audience and your customers. If they comment on a social media posting, respond. If the comments are positive, thank them and let them know they're appreciated. And if the comments are negative, apologize, be sincere and let them know what steps the business is taking to make the necessary changes. Allow your social media follows to post feedback on your platforms so other users will be able to see. Be transparent and audiences will resonate more with the business.

Find the keywords to SEO your website

Once the basics of your site have been established, all that is left to do is lay the foundation for successful Search Engine Optimization (SEO) in the future. The better the SEO of your site, the better your search engine ranking which means the more new potential customers you can bring in without actively seeking them out. To get started you will want to go to the Setting menu, found from the Dashboard, and choose the option titled Home.

Here you will want to include a title, a detailed description using keywords of your chose as well as the Meta keywords that will ultimately be displayed. The title should be short and sweet while still including your primary keyword and should always be fewer than 60 total characters. Your Meta description is what will be seen when your site is shown via a search engine, you need to be concise as you only have 160 characters to work with here. Finally, you will want to include specific keywords separated by commas. If you aren't quite sure which keywords to use, consider the following tips to ensure you are headed in the right direction:

Start by checking with Google: As the primary way that new potential customers will be stumbling upon your content, it makes sense that Google is also the first place to look for relevant keywords. All you need to do is enter the name of your general niche into the search bar and see what options fill in automatically. It is important to take note of what comes up both while you are typing the phrase and after you have included it in its entirety. These can be considered the major topics that people turn to when it comes to your niche so it will typically behoove you to include them in your site.

Once you are done at the top of the page, scroll down to the bottom of the first page of results for a list of other searches that are related to the search you have just finished conducting. While all of these may not be related to your take on the niche in question, they should still give you a few useful takeaways as well as ideas for how to logically expand your site in the future. Your goal from this exercise should be to come up with approximately 5 strong keywords to base your SEO strategy around, having too many keywords will only hurt you in the long run so it is important to narrow your choices down right away.

Consider what Wikipedia thinks: Additionally, you will want to visit Wikipedia to determine what it thinks are the most relevant keywords to your niche. Wikipedia has become one of the top ranked websites across the entire world without putting a single cent into advertising and this is solely because they really know what they are doing when it comes to maximizing their SEO. Start by typing your nice into the search bar, if it brings up a direct result great, otherwise add the name of whatever page it links to your list of words.

From there you will want to consider the first paragraph overview of the content in question. This paragraph generally provides a brief glimpse at the content of the article in general complete with every possible link to additional content that could be relevant to the search in question. Depending on your take on the niche, every single one of those words could be used in your keyword search, the hard part is narrowing them down.

The search function on your site: While this won't necessarily be useful right off the bat, once your site has been around long enough to start drawing in some traffic, pouring over your own search data will show you the types of things that people who visit your site are looking for with no ifs and or buts. You can find these results from your Google Analytics page and using this information to improve your SEO is highly recommended once you have the opportunity to do so.

More Google: Google Correlate, available at Google.com/ Trends/Correlate can help you to more easily determine what related topics the people interested in your niche are also interested in. For example, if your niche is related to outdoor exploration then you might find that people who are interested in outdoor exploration are also interested in survival prepping. Not only will the program show you just which keywords are searched in related searches but also just how often each of those searches was performed. The program even breaks down the usage of specific keywords to various geographic locations, allowing you to pinpoint the particular interests of your audience even more readily.

Don't forget Amazon: Once you have an idea of what keywords tend to show up the most reliably in SEO rankings, the other type of keywords you will want to consider are those which are searched on Amazon which means they are the keywords people use when they are ready to buy something. As visitors who are primed to buy should be your primary concern, using these keywords can hook in the visitors with the appropriate mindset. To make use of this process simply type in your nice and see what types of items it points you towards. Again it is important to not simply spam keywords but add in useful ones to broaden your reach.

Soovle: While your goal should be to home in on fewer than 10 keywords, by this point you should be pretty close to that number. To round out your list you should consider visiting

253

soovle.com. This site brings together all of the related keyword information from Amazon.com, Yahoo.com, Bing.com YouTube.com, Answers.com, and Wikipedia.com but it is important to not simply start here as the wide variety of information available can make it difficult to determine the true best keywords for the task at hand.

Once you have run your niche through the Soovle search engine, look through the results and find the perfect few to cap off your list of keywords. What you should be looking for at this point is not specific words but general themes amongst the searches that the various results provide, themes to searches are more valuable than individual keywords as they encompass a wider variety of topics.

Chapter 4: Be Yourself

While many people on social media who are looking to make it big make the mistake of trying to be like everyone else, it is instead far better to spend time highlighting what makes you special. Your social media followers are going to be drawn to whatever it is about you that makes you unique, rather than trying to hide it (whatever it is) you should be looking for ways to flaunt it.

Find your voice

The voice that you speak to your user makes a really big difference. You can't switch voices all the time either. You need to find a voice and stick to it. Generally speaking, there are two styles of voice you can take on and experience moderate success with. These are friendly and authoritative. They can be marked by their differences in tone and approachability, and they both have their own specific use instances.

Friendly voices should be used when you're doing something more casual and you're trying to appeal to a more general audience. For example, the Paleo diet blog would optimally be written in a friendly voice as opposed to an authoritative voice, because the friendly voice will appeal to more people.

It doesn't sound scholarly and it doesn't sound out of its element; it just sounds like you're casually writing about something you care about, and that goes a long way when it comes to pulling people in towards your idea. Friendly voices will use a lot more slang and casual expressions than authoritative voices do, but they also can come off as less domineering. This can be good or it can be bad, again depending upon your niche. You will sound less secure in what you're doing, naturally, because you won't be using as confident of phrasing – authoritative voice, by its very nature, is more "confident" because it's sparser and to the point, both of which factor into people taking the voice seriously. However, more people will enjoy reading your blog and treat it as less of a manual, which means that you appeal to a more general audience.

Authoritative voices should be used when you're doing something that is gravely serious or perhaps even dangerous, when you're trying to appeal to a more bookish niche, or when you're trying to come off as more serious. For example, an affiliate marketing blog that was dedicated to maintaining high-mileage cars would benefit from using an authoritative voice because you have a specific enough niche that you aren't trying to appeal to more people or sound more "cool" or "open"; you're simply trying to give the impression that your way is the right way, and that whatever you do is generally the right way to do it.

When you're doing the authoritative voice, your main concern is that you come across as if you know what you're doing to the end user. This is your whole intent here. You aren't going to win over crowds with this, but then again, that's not your game anyway. Your game is getting people involved with your very specific niche and thinking that you're the guy to go to for everything.

Know your tone

While you should already know what type of content your target audience will be expecting, the way in which you present this information is going to be equally vital when it comes to showing them that you are just alike, except for the fact that you know more than they do. To accomplish this task, you are going to want to make an extra effort to get into their minds, speak as they speak, think like they think and use the same references that they use to relate to one another. The easiest way to do so is to consult your demographic data and pick the largest section of it to adopt as your own.

If your target audience is under 30 then the best way to ensure that you are all on the same page is to visit YouTube.com and listen to the current tastemakers on the niche in question. If you have a niche that is focused more on those over 30, then the time you spent studying the niche should be enough to push you in the right direction. Assuming your target audience is younger, then you will want to watch videos made by content creators with the most views as this shows that they are doing something that the target audience really responds to. Understanding the sound of your target audience will make your claim to authority more believable because you will sound like a peer rather than a researcher.

Additionally, you will want to consider what, aside from being an authority, you are trying to convince your target audience of and what you are trying to get them to do. The more precise your response is, the more effectively you can ensure it comes out the content you create. Furthermore, you may find that it is helpful to consider the values, atmosphere, and culture that you are trying to cultivate and how you can make those things come through your content as well.

Be more confident

When it comes to sharing every facet of yourself on social media, it is important to keep in mind that no matter what you do, you need to do so with confidence. Confidence is something that lots of people want, but few people know how to go about acquiring. This issue is often magnified by the fact that those who are typically perceived as confident often can't clearly articulate what it is about them that makes them this way. This is because being confident is a habit which means there are simple, effective, things you can do to ensure this trait becomes a habit.

While thinking about the many ways you could be more confident in the future is easy, it does little when it comes to actually doing anything to change your current persona. Unfortunately, moving in a positive direction is far more difficult than simply thinking about doing so and the only thing that mitigates this is the fact that stepping out of your comfort zone for the first time is tricky, and potentially terrifying for everyone who first sets out to try it. The good news is that if you persevere it will get easier every time you do it. To help you deal with the initial hardship, keep the following in mind:

Be aware of your strengths and weaknesses: If you are ever going to be confident in yourself enough to change for the better, you are going to need to look within and have a frank discussion with yourself about what you find. This means taking an honest look at not just your strengths, but all your flaws and weaknesses as well. While it might seem rather basic, the reality of the situation is that a solid round of self-analysis will do you some good, no matter what type of larger changes you are looking to make.

The best way to get started knowing yourself more intimately is to find a large mirror somewhere private and then stand in front of it completely naked. While many people will no doubt consider this a literal version of torture, persevering through the initial moments of discomfort is sure to lead to a number of surprising revelations. First and foremost, among them is that you likely don't look nearly as bad as the mental picture that you have in your head might indicate. The reality might very well be worse in some situations, but likely better in others as well. Regardless, the only way you can ever expect to mount a charge for change is by knowing exactly where you need to launch the first attack.

When it comes to making changes that are sure to boost your confidence levels, you will want to start with areas that are going to cause you to see the greatest overall difference in the shortest period of time possible. This may mean cutting back on a few troubling foods or it could be the start of a major dietary and exercise trend, the specifics don't matter, what does is that you make a concentrated effort to change and stick with it in the long term. Even if you are lucky enough to only need to tighten things up a little bit, make a point of going out and getting a nice haircut or buying some new clothes, making an effort at this stage is a key part of making any future changes stick.

Play the odds: If you never try, you'll never succeed. If instead of running from every opportunity to display self-confidence, you seek out as many of them as you can find, statistically speaking, you can't fail every single time. Until you make it more of a daily habit, being self-confident is a numbers game. The more you play the odds, the more you're likely to come up a winner.

Take the time to decide why you are really afraid: If you find yourself always responding to situations that require self-confidence in the same fearful pattern. Consider this, the human mind loves to find patterns, even when no true pattern exists. This means you may be responding to an established pattern and not actually the specifics of the current situation.

259

The next time you begin to feel scared or nervous prior to having to exhibit self-confidence, take the extra moment to consider your current situation and see what it is that is really making you feel that way. If nothing specific presents itself, then the odds are good that your mind is instead reacting to a pattern that doesn't really exist.

Stop thinking about it: Thinking about all the ways that being more self-confident will help you in the future may take your mind off the present, but it won't do much to get you started when it comes to improving your day-to-day interactions with others. At some point, you need to put your new and improved thoughts into actions.

While stretching your comfort zone will be difficult at first, the fact that it is just as difficult for everyone else to do the same should make those first few steps easier. While it may be hard to believe, the only real difference between you and those with the self-confidence that you admire is that when confronted with their initial obstacles, they overcame. All you need to do is follow their example.

Stick with it: When it comes to working on turning confidence into a habit, you may find that simply writing down "I am confident" 10 times each day goes a long way towards helping you find success. As you do so, consider all the ways that being confident would improve your day-to-day life and also all the ways that you are improving your confidence over time. Don't just think about the differences that even more confidence would make in your life, really imagine that they are real. Write this list on a small piece of paper in the morning and then carry it with you throughout the day so you can ensure some part of your thoughts are on improving your confidence.

Chapter 5: Find Your Audience

Niche considerations

In order to get repeat traffic and get people constantly visiting, you're going to need to attract people with a certain interest. You'll have to pinpoint that interest and start making posts that are geared towards that specific interest. This is your niche: the area of interest that you decide to take advantage of and post about.

The best way to make a lot of money is for your niche to be something you care about enough to go back to every day. This is going to drive you to work on it and constantly produce content. If you don't care about your niche then it's going to show through in your posts. You can expect some amount of return, but they will almost certainly not be great. Bear that in mind as you go forward.

There are a few different ways to go about picking the perfect niche. The first is the hardest: go off of your passions. If you do this, you're going to have to find innovative ways using products that affiliate companies offer, if they don't have any for your specific niche. However, this can pay off by you making really creative and potentially viral posts using things in unconventional ways that people will see as super intriguing. This is a good way to bring in a whole bunch of people.

In order to do this, you're going to need to be very crafty and keep an eye on what's available. Additionally, a lot of your income will be coming through other means mentioned in this book rather than affiliate marketing. However, it's an option worth considering because affiliate marketing can almost certainly play a part in a strategy like this one.

The second is the easiest, but you're playing the odds in two respects. The second method is to simply see what products and avenues are available to you through affiliate marketing channels and then derive your niche from that. In some cases, this will intertwine with the first concept and you'll find something that you're both passionate about and that there are a fair number of products for which you can market. However, this won't always be the case.

In the event that you can't find something you're reasonably passionate about, simply try to find something that you're somewhat interested in or would like to learn more about for yourself. This will make it easier to research and find topics related to it that you're interested in.

However, sometimes you just won't be able to find anything that interests you. In these cases, you can still just go with whatever you think would do fairly well. Sometimes intuition can be a really important thing, and in these cases, you should just trust your intuition in trying to find a pertinent niche through affiliate marketing channels.

In some ways, this is the best way to start affiliate marketing if you want your focus to be solely affiliate marketing, or at least primarily so. This is because you'll know going into it what mechanisms and products you can try to take advantage of when trying to pull in customers and users.

Another way to figure out your niche is simply to use keywords in order to learn what topics are hot right now. This might give you the most instantaneous benefit, but you will inevitably find it rather difficult to carry this out for a long period of time because trends are constantly changing. You'll most likely find success using this method in the short run (if you can write some great articles and take advantage of available affiliate marketing opportunities) but you'll find it difficult to maintain that same level of success in the long run.

That's not to say that your posts when using this method will ever be worthless. Quite the opposite, you're fairly likely to make a decent amount off of this even after the bubble bursts on whatever trend you're taking advantage of. However, it is worth bearing in mind that this is not a great tactic to use when you're trying to make a great-quality and long-lasting site. You may find yourself having difficulties coming up with a good topic down the line, especially if your given trend is particularly niche.

If you do decide to take this avenue, however, all you'll have to do is get access to popular keywords and figure out what's trending. The easiest way to do this is probably to take advantage of Google Trends. Simply Google "Google trends hot trends" and the page you're looking for should be relatively easy to find. This will tell you the most trending topics of the day every hour or so. It's generally the top 20.

However, this can be rather unwieldy, as it won't exactly tell you the sort of information you want to write a book about. After all, these are just the most trending searches for the last day or so, and they generally on very specific people and events rather than topics you can easily write a book about.

It's for this reason that you may wish to check other sources for keywords. Unfortunately, eBooks frown a bit upon including links, but there are numerous services that a simple Google search should readily return!

Tips for success: If, when looking at your life through the filter of potential niches you aren't finding anything that automatically stands out, odds are you aren't looking closely enough. If this is the case then you will want to go through your daily routine with an eye towards what you do on the regular that is popular enough to have a built-in audience while at the same time not so popular that you won't be able to carve out your own unique space in the niche.

Once you have a list of potential topics you will then want to break them down into more specific categories, 2 per topic should be enough, and then do a little bit of online research to see how well the space is currently defined by existing websites. They won't all be winners, and many of them might not even be profitable, but the exercise should be enough to get the juices flowing and reveal great niche potential that was hiding in plain sight.

If you still can't seem to find the right niche to target, but you know what type of product or service you are trying to market, then you may find it useful to visit Amazon.com and check in on the products you are interested in selling or those related to the service you are going to provide. These products will then be classified into categories, each of which is ripe with potential niches and sub-niches.

Narrow down your search

Find the right target: Once you have a number of potentially profitable niches to consider, the next thing you will want to do in order to cull them down to the best ones possible is to consider what type of potential customers you are interested in targeting. Finding your target audience can be done in several different ways, starting with consider your own demographic and considering if people like you would be interested in your product or service.

Like with the niche itself, it is important to focus on a fairly specific segment of the purchasing population as each target group is going to have very different likes and dislikes. For example, if you go too broad with your category you may land on men, but a student who isn't yet old enough to drink is going to have dramatically different priorities than a 40-year-old family man. If you decide to go to broad on your target audience you will only end up creating content that doesn't really appeal to anyone.

Understand the problems that they face: Once you have a specific demographic in mind, the next thing that you are going to want to spend some time thinking about is the problems that the demographic faces on a regular basis. Additionally, you are going to want to consider the aspirations and desires that they have and the issues that might confront them when it comes to making their dreams a reality. Once you have done some brainstorming, the next thing you will want to do is to head back to Google and plug in the words you have come up with to see what the general online space regarding them looks like. If the problems you come up with don't see many results then it isn't really a problem your target audience is concerned with.

Know if it is profitable: Once you have landed on several different problems that your target audience is interested in solving, you will then need to determine if they are willing to pay to solve the problem in question as otherwise, it won't be worth the time and effort involved to market content when it won't lead to a measurable number of sales. The easiest way to do this is to visit Adwords.Google.com and check out the keyword planner tool. This tool will allow you to view search

265

results filtered by various keywords to determine how frequently they are used. You will not only be able to see how frequently the keyword is searched for but also what the breakdown is like month to month and how easily it is for people to find the information that they are looking for.

With these details in mind, you are then going to want to visit several of the sites that already exist around the topic in order to meet the current demand for information. While on these sites it is important to look for those that have an active advertising base outside of Google AdSense. Anyone can sign up for advertising via Google, but if the site has actual companies advertising on it then you know that there is definitely money to be made from the community.

Go deep: Outside of understanding the problems that your target audience faces on a regular basis, you are also going to need to consider the ways in which they work to solve these problems. As an example, if you are looking to target individuals who are looking for soulmates then you are going to want to consider what exactly that phrase means to them, the qualities that they look for in a romantic partner and even how they approach the idea of love in general.

This deep dive into the psyche of your future target audience is going to help you to learn how they think which is crucial when it comes to creating the type of content that they are going to enjoy. Additionally, it will help you to understand the language that they use amongst themselves including common lingo and current slang. Only by understanding them inside and out will you be able to create the type of content that will speak to them enough to generate the types of results that they are looking for.

Determine if you can go the distance: After you have found a niche that you believe that will work for you, it is important to have an honest conversation with yourself in order to determine if you are going to actually have the ability to provide this niche the type of quality content that is going to get you the results that you are looking for. You are going to want to be able to do more than just create random stray bits of content, you are going to need to create an entire story around what you are doing and make it believable to those who are going to be in the easiest position to call you out if you are faking it.

Be aware of industry trends: Just because a given niche currently has what appears to be a thriving audience base doesn't mean that you are going to want to jump in right away without some additional research. This is because it is entirely possible that the niche you have chosen has already peaked in popularity so that despite your best efforts it is extremely likely that there will be fewer and fewer customers to be interested in your content as time goes on.

The trend tool from Google is extremely useful in this instance as it shows how often a keyword was searched in a given month. Specifically, in this instance, you are going to want to target niches where the number of searches is each monthly is always on the rise as opposed to those where the biggest surge of search popularity has already peaked.

Consider if you will be able to find a way in: Once you have managed to find a few likely niches, the next thing you will want to do is to determine if there is currently enough room in the niche for your unique spin on the content. Once more you will want to visit Google and do a simple search utilizing the types of keywords that your target audience is likely going to use. The types of results that you are looking for are those which feature a wide variety of different sites as opposed to those that only feature a handful of different websites. The fewer different search results that show up on the first page, the less likely it will be that you are able to break into the market.

Generate content ideas: Once you have done the research to come up with 2 or 3 different potentially profitable niches or sub-niches that you are interested in pursuing in a real way, the final thing that you will want to do is to take the time to determine if you have enough ideas to generate enough content to get you started. Specifically, you are going to want to come up with around 50 different topics that you will be able to create content of some sort around in addition to half again as many social media posts that you can use to keep things flowing while you are working on generating your blog posts or video.

When you first get started you are going to want to post around 3 different pieces of content a week so the 50 that you come up with to start should be enough to get you through the first month. While you can slow down after you have built up your content archive, you won't want to slow down too much, ideally, you should keep up the habit of posting at least 2 new pieces of content every week. If you can't come up with at least 50 topics from the start you are going to want to go back to the drawing board as it is a sure sign that you are going to have difficulty keeping up the content stream on a continual basis. While you may not like the idea of starting over again from scratch it is vastly preferable to going through all the work of starting a content marketing program and then having to scrap it all because you have run out of content.

Niches to get you started

While certain topics are going to be a flash in the pan, starting off strong before fizzling out sooner than later, others are going to be evergreen and will always have a target audience waiting to consume new content. For the best results, start with one of these and then look for a relatively new sub-niche that you can really put your mark on.

Wealth, health and romance: Known in the content marketing world as the big 3, wealth, health and romance niches are always popular and new sub-niches are always popping up to give them a boost as well. What's more, the target audience for each has long been trained to always be on the lookout for the next big thing which means you will have a group of individuals who are eager to throw money at your product or service. Essentially this means that there are potential customers beyond count out there that are just waiting for someone new (you and your content) to tell them how to solve all their problems and they are willing to throw as much money at the issue as it takes to find the happiness they are looking for.

The health niche is full of sub-niches including things like smoking cessation, medical ailments, weight loss trends and helps with embarrassing personal problems like hair loss or IBS. The wealth niche includes plenty of evergreen sub-niches as well including things like affiliate marketing, multilevel marketing, internet marketing, gambling and investment markets such as forex or options trading. Finally, the romance sub-niche includes things like finding a romantic partner, pick up tricks, online dating, attraction tips and reconnecting with a former partner.

High-end hobbies: If you are interested in a niche that is somewhat less predatory than one of the evergreen three listed above, then choosing a niche that is devoted to an expensive hobby is a great way to ensure that you will always be able to find new products and services to sell. From horseback riding to marijuana, if you can come up with a somewhat unique spin to give your content a little boost you can be sure that people with expensive hobbies are always going to be lining up to learn about the next big thing. If you are afraid that you may not have enough ideas to ensure a steady stream of new content, then choosing a niche based around an expensive hobby may be the way to go.

Chapter 6: Create an Offer

The next step in building your personal brand, making sales, and defining your target audience is creating a customized offer for the audience you previously identified. This customized offer should be based on everything you learned about your audience, supporting you in creating an offer that directly supports them in having their needs met. This means that they are more likely to be interested in your offer, thus helping you maximize your engagement and make sales right off the bat.

This offer is going to do three things for you: increase exposure, earn sales, and perform market research. Through this offer, you are going to have people purchasing from you as long as you have crafted it correctly based on your demographic. The most important aspect of all of this, however, is that you are going to see exactly who within your overall demographic is actually purchasing what you are creating for them.

This particular demographic will be far more defined, making them the ones you want to cater to. For example, if you know that moms in their 20s and 30s are your primary demographic but that moms between the ages of 28-34 who have more than one kid are your biggest purchasing audience, then you know specifically who you want to cater your brand toward. This goes for any audience. The more defined audience will be drawn not from those who engage the most, but from those who are actually willing to purchase from you.

If you are not yet ready to make sales, you might consider making a free offer that allows people to join you in an online live event, download something you have made for them, or otherwise engage with you in a way that requires for them to actually commit to something. This particular will not earn you money, nor will it give you an exact idea of who is willing to pay for your content versus who is simply willing to accept the free offer, but it will give you a stronger idea of the demographic you are targeting. This is a great idea if you are not yet ready to design an offer or if you are still trying to navigate the waters in which you are wading.

Getting started: To start, you will want to put a face to your potential client (download a photo from the internet that identifies the physical characteristics of your potential customer) and a fictitious name. Next, you will want to compile the data that will trace the characteristics of sociodemographic, psychographic and consumer experiences. This serves to have a clear representation of him/her with whom you are going to talk and with whom you should want to relate.

This exercise can lead to a great transformation to your company; in fact, it will help you understand the motivating beliefs, fears, and secret desires that influence the purchase decisions of the customer and tunes your marketing efforts and understand what solutions to offer to your market.

A great resource to boost this process and find people that meet your avatar standards on Facebook is lookup-id.com. Thanks to this website, you can define your target customer through the definition of personal characteristics and get a list of people that met them.

Once that you have entered the website, go on the "extract members" section. It is very easy to find on the top right of the page. From there, you want to insert the ID of a Facebook group in your niche, which of course will contain people in line with your offer. The website will give you a complete and detailed list of the people in the group, which means that you have just discovered a goldmine since those will be interested in what you are offering.

On this website, you can even use the FB Search function. Once you have designed the features of your typical prospect, you can insert them in this platform to get a list of users that meet those standards. It is pretty straight forward and it is very easy to use.

Be aware of value propositions

In order to craft the most compelling value proposition possible, it is important to look at your business as well as your brand in an analytical fashion. For starters, this means that you are going to want to clearly and succinctly explain what it is you do in just a few simple phrases. For example, if your website sells clothes and generates quality content on the importance of personal style, you might explain your business as one that sells shoes as well as providing training and coaching that promotes personal flair.

The next thing you will want to consider is what problem your business solves, ideally one that not all of your competition solves as well. To continue with the clothing example, perhaps you help clients express their personalities, sell clothing that is low maintenance, caters to your niche in one way or another or simply provide options that are difficult to find elsewhere. If you are having a hard time deciding what problems you solve and which you want to focus on when it comes to maximizing your value propositions, a good place to go for inspirations are the reviews that clients leave about your products. Depending on the severity of the problem that you are helping to solve, this type of information is often prominently displayed and can ensure you are focusing in the direction that your target audience will appreciate.

Once you understand what problem you solve, the next thing you will need to consider is what value clients have gained once they have completed their business with you. This is more than just the product or service that you provide, it is the true value that lurks somewhere within your product or service. With this in mind, you are going to want to consider various promises that you can make to elucidate this value in a way that is relevant to the problem you solve. Additionally, it needs to be specific in that it clearly explains the value you provide and the timeframe in which you solve the problem you target. Finally, it should be something that is relatively unique to your business which makes you the obvious choice when compared to even your closest competition.

Consider affiliate opportunities

Affiliate marketing is one of the most common entry points for many people into the world of running a business online and it is easy to see why. Essentially, all you have to do is to promote the products that other people are selling and if you do your job well enough, you make a commission each time someone you sent to the product page in question actually follows through and buys the product in question. It really is that simple, all you need to do is find a product you like, talk about why you like it in a way that is compelling for others and then give your viewers an easy way to purchase the product you like for themselves.

There are two main sides to any affiliate marketing equation, the creator of the product and the primary seller of the product are on one side and the person doing the affiliate marketing is on the other. With this in mind, it is easy to see affiliate marketing as spreading the benefits of product creation as well as the marketing of products across a range of different group where each group receives a slice of one whole financial pie according to their individual contributions.

Broadly referred to as the merchant, the seller, vendor, retailer or creator of the product all ultimately fit into this category and all have a product that they need help selling. This need is met by the affiliate who can also be called a publisher, this can be a single person or even an entire company devoted to either helping to sell a single product or a large variety of them. This marketing can be done in several different ways, perhaps the most common of which is a website reviewing a specific brand of products. Instead of focusing on a single brand, the affiliate website could also simply catalog items that theoretically appeal to a specific buying audience.

This buying audience is what matters the most to affiliate marketers as consumers are the key to the whole affiliate marketing process. Without actual paying customers, affiliate marketers are not earning commissions and merchants are stuck sitting on unsold goods. While the consumer is definitely part of a successful affiliate marketing cycle, the amount they are aware of the process is typically left up to the affiliate marketer in question. Regardless of the level of transparency, the sales are still counted in the same way and generate the same amount of commission.

The final participant in many affiliate marketing cycles is the network that is used to connect the merchant with the affiliate marketer in question. While some marketers are known to work without networks, setting up revenue sharing plans with merchants directly, the majority use a third party to worry about handling payments and product delivery concerns. Networks are also a great place for new affiliate marketers to find out about product marketing opportunities that they may otherwise miss.

Currently worth an estimated 6.5 billion dollars, the affiliate marketing industry first began in 1994 by a man named William J Tobin, for his website PC Flowers & Gifts. In 1995 they had more than 2,500 affiliate marketers on the burgeoning Internet and Tobin obtained a patent on the idea in early 1996. That same year, Amazon.com launched an affiliate program to allow people to receive credit for linking to their listings for various books. This affiliate program is still around today, called Amazon Associates, this network now allows any potential marketers to promote any item which they sell.

Platforms

Affiliate marketing platforms are large marketplaces where merchants and affiliates can meet and interact. The platform then takes a percentage of each commission that the affiliate makes. In return, the platform aggregates all of the offers currently available creates an easily searchable database and handles the task of finding new merchants. All platforms are not created equal, however, take a look at the list below and find the platform that is right for you.

ShareASale: This large affiliate marketing platform currently has more than 4,000 unique merchants and nearly 30 percent are unique to ShareASale. They are well liked by the community for the large amount of information they have on the current commission rates their merchants are paying including average commission, average sale amount, average reversal rats and average earnings per click. While these are averages, not guarantees, it can certainly give you an idea of what to shoot for moving forward.

Additional advantages include a rapid turnaround time of monthly payments for everyone with a balance of more than $50 and a comparison tool that makes it easy to find the merchants who are paying the best rates in a specific niche. On the other hand, the reporting database that affiliates use to track their results is clunkier and harder to use than some of the alternatives.

CJ Affiliate: Another extremely large affiliate platform, this platform will have practically every single merchant who runs an affiliate program that you can imagine including different levels of exposure which allows you to find the choice that fits your site the best. They also make it easy to find relevant affiliate tracking codes and make it easy to get started marketing the type of content you are comfortable within just a handful of hours.

Their biggest benefit is their wealth of reporting options which makes it easy to know where your most profitable posts are hiding. It is more complicated to use, however, so it is not for everyone.

Rakuten Linkshare: Rakuten Linkshare has been around much longer than your average affiliate platform which means it can be counted on for reliable affiliate programs and a broad range of merchants. One of their most unique features is being able to cycle through multiple banners for a single product automatically. It also offers a wider range of options for connecting to the merchant page of your choice than many of the other platforms.

Amazon Associates: The biggest online retailer in the world, Amazon has the affiliate program to match. While their commissions are going to be smaller, the range of products they offer is such that everyone eventually comes around and forms an Amazon Associate account.

Clickbank: Another of the oldest platforms around, Clickbank was formed at the tail end of the last century and has been innovating in the space ever since. It primarily focuses on products of the digital information variety with over 6 million products being offered through affiliate programs for merchants all around the world.

eBay: While many affiliate marketers may not even be aware that eBay offers an affiliate program, in reality, they are surprisingly competitive. eBay has over 150 million active users and practically everyone has an eBay account. What's more, posts that link to eBay auctions look even less like advertisements than those that contain more traditional links. Their affiliate tools allow affiliates to create unique links to any item they choose as well as offering tracking of individual results. The biggest downside, of course, is that unlike many other types of affiliate programs you have to curate your listings more regularly as items will frequently be going out of stock.

Advangate: This platform focuses primarily on online services and digital goods including more than 23,000 software titles. They also offer some of the highest blanket commission rates around with even new affiliates earning commissions of up to 75 percent of the price of the software in question. They provide a wide variety of tools to ensure affiliates are getting the most out of their time and pay out on a monthly basis. The biggest downside is that most of the software is fairly technical in nature so it will take more research than it might otherwise to see the best results.

FlexOffers: This site offers a number of physical and online-only merchants with numerous brands that are mainstream as well as those appealing to certain niches. What sets FlexOffers apart is that they have a team of editors and writers who are regularly producing quality copy that those who are not comfortable writing their own would simply need to change somewhat before posting. These reviews even come with all of the links in place. Their rates are not as competitive as some of the other platforms, however, which is why those who can write their own posts might consider doing so.

Avantlink: Avantlink has made a name for itself thanks to its above-average tracking programs as well as their above average customer support that makes them a great choice for new affiliate marketers who want to be able to easily speak with a real person when it comes time to ask questions. They also offer some of the most in-depth tracking when it comes to following similar products over a period of time. They offer country-specific networks in the UK, Canada, and the United States which can limit their affiliate potential in some cases.

RevenueWire: With over 1 billion leads generated, RevenueWire offers affiliates a wide range of merchants from more than 200 countries who focus mainly on digital services in several languages. They also offer new affiliate marketers a personal account manager who will work with you to form the right marketing plan for the niche you have in mind. They also allow affiliates to form and run their own affiliate networks to

279

gain access to even more opportunities. If you are looking for something with a broader focus, or something not quite so hands-on, you might want to look elsewhere.

Tips for success

While producing the right type of content, day in and day out, and doing everything you can to ensure your audience remains interested, is a crucial part of profiting from social media, it is obviously not the end. Rather, it is just a means to generate conversions as you can have the best content in your niche but it will all come to nothing if you don't have the ability to capitalize fully on all those unadulterated page views. In order to guarantee that all your hard work pays off, consider these tips.

Set goals early: First things first, it is important to remember that there is more to successful content marketing than bringing people to your site for the first time. As such, you are going to decide if you are looking to improve your rate of mentions on social media, mentions of your brand, increasing your email newsletter metrics, improving where you show up on Google, or even improving your views overall to increase ad revenue, just to name a few. The exact goal you are working towards doesn't matter, what does matter is that you need to have it clearly in mind moving forward so that you can track your results properly and find real success.

In order to track your goals successfully, you are going to need to consider the metrics that have the most relevance in the situation:

- When tracking brand mentions, you are going to want to keep an eye on the share of voice metric. This can be done via a social mentions tool which can measure how frequently a given brand is mentioned based on the relevant industry average.

- When improving your Google ranking you are going to want to employee niche specific SEO tools to get you where you need to be.

- In order to track your social media presence successfully, web traffic or product sales you can find the relative metrics for each from the backend of your website.

Regardless of which metrics you are keeping an eye on, you can't ever expect to see any realistic growth unless you keep a close eye on your metrics at all times.

SMART goals

When it comes to creating your first offer, it can be easy to try and reach for the stars in an effort to court as many potential customers as possible. Instead of going overboard with your offer, it is important to first consider the goals you have for it, and the best way to ensure that your goals are on point is to ensure that they are SMART.

Specific: It is important to always have a specific, clear goal in mind whenever you set out to accomplish something new. The foggier the goal, the easier it will be for your mind to come up with excuses to do something more immediately satisfying instead. Having something specific in mind instead gives you something to focus on when your mind starts putting forth excuses. Know your goal and focus on it when times get tough and you will find it easier to power through the right way.

For example, the goal: "having an offer that is successful" is too vague to provide the direct motivation you need to be effective, a more proactive goal would be to find an offer that improves your conversions by 25 percent in a specific period of time. The first goal is vague enough that excuses can slip through the cracks, the second has a specific success/fail state that leaves little in the way of wiggle room.

If you aren't sure if your goal is specific enough, run through the 5Ws and H: who, what, where, why, when and how. If your goal is specific enough that you can determine who will be involved, what will be accomplished, where it will be accomplished, why you are doing it, when you will start working on it and how you will see it through then you are likely on the right track.

Measurable: SMART goals are measurable. When it comes to choosing the goals that you are going to set for yourself, it is important that what you choose has a degree of success that is associated with it. Only by understanding when you have done poorly will you even be able to realistically hope to improve. There are many scenarios that can arise that will find you feeling as though you are making progress when in reality you are doing little more than spinning your wheels, and setting measurable goals will help prevent you from finding yourself in this scenario.

The best way to keep your goals measurable is to set up a generalized time table based on whatever it is that you have planned for yourself and then keep track of how you are doing in relation to it. This time table won't need to be extremely precise, as long as it has specific deadlines that you can always actively be working towards, then it is doing its job. Keeping tabs on your success in chunks will ensure that you not only start off on the right foot but keep that success up all the way through to the finish line as well.

Attainable: A good goal is not only specific and measurable; it is realistically attainable as well. All the planning and measuring in the world will never do you any good if you have decided to work towards a goal that is never going to be able to be achieved, no matter what. While setting a goal to be a billionaire might help motivate you to try great things, if you are not already well on your way then it is too pie in the sky to realistically attempt to approach at the moment. If the goal you are working for doesn't seem realistically attainable you will find it much harder to focus on it with the real determination you are going to need to see any goal through to completion, making it even more unlikely you are going to be able to attain it still. Stick with goals that remain in the realm of possibility for the best results.

Relevant: When it comes to setting goals to improve your offers, it is important that you start with goals that will have the most noticeable effect on your day to day life at first, and then work towards more abstract goals from there. This type of approach will have numerous benefits in both the short and the long term, ultimately culminating in a mental state that is clear of distractions and more accurately able to focus on the long term results you need to see true financial freedom.

When you are first starting out, choosing goals that will have the most immediate impact on your current situation will not only make it easier to focus on other tasks down the line once the current distractions are out of the way, it will also teach your brain to associate hard work and dedication with successfully completing goals. This, in turn, will make it easier for you to commit to more difficult or complicated goals in the long term as you will have a historical reason to equate hard work and dedication with success.

Timely: While you won't be able to tell a proper SMART goal apart from the rest by just looking at a few of its properties, you will always be able to identify one by its strict timetable including a firm start and finish date. Ultimately it will not matter how measurable, specific, relevant and attainable your goal is as without a firm timeframe for you to complete it in, the odds of it actually seeing completion drop below 20 percent.

It is important that you don't take from this the fact that no timeline is malleable, as it is perfectly natural for timelines to change as new data regarding the goal is uncovered. The important thing is then to ensure that you are not moving your goals for the wrong reasons and only updating things based on hard facts that previously were only guessed at using anecdotal information. It is important to do as much research as possible before setting a firm goal and then to only change it when it turns out that your initial information is wrong, never for internal reasons related purely to giving yourself more time to goof off and avoid doing what needs to be done.

Chapter 7: Staying on Brand on Facebook

Facebook groups

A Facebook group is a micro-community within the largest community of the network that, focusing on specific themes, attracts specific segments of a given niche. Unlike pages, in fact, groups have a greater predisposition to the generation of discussions and not to a simple unilateral posting of content. What does this mean? Simple: that the posts on the groups will have greater visibility and the possibility to reach more easily your target audience.

Finding the right group: Let us imagine, of course, that you have already identified the niche or sector on which to base your communication strategy. The first of the problems you need to solve is to find groups to distribute your content on.

The best place to start is with a simple search, you can use the search bar to find groups that meet your requirements. For example, if you look for a group that deals with cooking, you can type "cooking" into the search bar and then apply the filter "groups" (Facebook will initially search among posts, people and so on).

If you want to narrow things down even more then you will want to use the Graph Search" option which makes it is possible to create more complex searches such as: "Groups joined by my friends who like cooking". That is: look for groups to which were added that part of your friends list who have indicated they enjoy cooking.

Create a network for your loyal fans: This group is made up of the most loyal fans, people who believe in your company, in your product, and in your values. Brands like Canva, who has a loyal fan base, called these groups "community groups" or "ambassador groups."

The one with the loyal fans is the most important group you can create on Facebook. It is important to create a positive word of mouth on your products, your company, and your activities. Be sure to make your fans feel special. You can do it in various ways; by sending out branded merchandise or by putting a comment regularly taking part in the conversation the group is having.

The most important thing is to thank them, heartily and regularly. A written note (maybe by hand), is much more pleasant than a thoughtless gift. Thank your fans for helping you grow your community and achieve your goals.

Here are some ways you can use these groups:

- Get feedback on new products. You have a new product to launch but first, you want to know how it would be accepted? This is the right place to test it.

- Attract new members. If your company has a membership program, this is a great way to keep in touch with them and attract new ones.

- Answer the questions. How many times have you seen a question on a group or an online forum and have you thought that your product could be the ideal solution? Of course, you could answer the question with your private profile, but you will be more successful by responding to the members of your group.

- Answer often to questions and to avoid spam (especially if there are many members in the group), tag two or three experts in the response that can respond appropriately.

- Recruit experts. Many people like to feel expert and be taken into consideration. And many like to share their knowledge with other people. Experienced people can help new consumers get closer to your product and buy it. Please note that it may be necessary to create a dedicated expert group.

Community pages

Pages that don't serve the purpose to represent anything or anyone, these pages are keen to wrap up wider niches of things, from basic trends to political drama. Usually, the subject of the page is something that can't be easily claimed by an enterprise or individual. For example, things like "Hot Dogs" or "Super Cute Dogs" or "Pride and Prejudice."

Community Pages, comparatively, are designed identically to Official Pages. These Pages tend to be more specific than their Topic counterparts, but the admins are not official representatives. You'll know you're looking at a Community Page if you see the word "Community" labeled directly below the cover photo.

Now, what does this all has to do with you? Simple, when you "like" anything, you're initiating a relationship with it that can be as "interactive" or as "hands-off" as you want it to be. Continuously, people like a lot of Pages simply as a signifier or badge on their Timelines.

On your page you're the master at the sail because you have the power to advertise as much and often as you like, you can guide others about advertising their businesses only on specified days of each week to get more and more interaction and page likes.

The most important thing you need to keep in mind is that groups never allow you to laser target users (leads) with your ads. However, you can, do this by using a "Page" even if you don't own a website for your business.

Video Ads

Facebook understands that people want different kinds of videos in different situations. For instance, if someone is on their mobile device, they are probably on-the-go and would prefer to watch something short. Meanwhile, if a person is on a larger device (like a laptop) and sitting on the couch, then they are likely more willing to watching a longer video.

For shorter videos, you might want to consider using in-feed ads. Whether your goal is to reinforce your brand or promote a new product, in-feed ads capitalize on quick, short spurts of attention from your target audience in order to promote your business.

Create a captivating video which quickly tells your story, and people, while scrolling through their feed, will stop to hear what your company has to say. Using video ads is a great way to drive sales. Furthermore, by combining video ads with product images and carousels, you can stimulate the interest of your audience and potentially increase your sales.

You can also create video ads that appear "in-stream," meaning the ad is shown after the viewer has begun watching a video.

In-stream video ads can be as long as fifteen seconds, but the shorter they are, the better. Research shows that 70 percent of in-stream ads are watched to completion, with the audio/sound on. This allows you to deliver a more dynamic message to your audience.

Another advantage of using video ads on Facebook is that it allows your company to reach people that you might not otherwise reach with more expensive television ads. Research shows that Facebook video ads reach 37 percent more people in the age group of 18 to 24. Facebook is also creating new ways of using video to engage your audience. With Facebook 360 your customers can interact with the video to explore a 3D or panoramic environment. This is particularly useful for businesses like Real Estate Agencies - instead of posting a picture of a house, they can create a 3D or Panoramic video of the interior of the house. This is much more eye-catching and attention-getting than a simple picture!

Finally, using Facebook Creative Hub, you can create "mock-up" or tester video ads, and then test them in real time.

Select the right placement to get a bigger reach: When you are working on a campaign on Facebook, you can choose from a variety of platforms, devices, and placements. This gives you a lot of choices and a lot of control over your campaign, and the best choice is going to depend on your goals and the type of campaign that you want to create.

One thing that you can try out is to add Instagram to the video view placement, the engagement, and the reach. This can improve your results by as much as 40 percent. However, when you do this, it is likely that you are going to see fewer comments and likes if you are running it as a Facebook page post ad.

You can also use Messenger here. It is a great add-on to traffic and the conversion campaign. Currently, Messenger ads are going to perform really well.

Audience Network placements are a great way to increase the traffic and reach for your ads in most cases. But you should pay some particular attention to the key metrics that you have. In some cases, you may want to run a campaign on one device because it can lower the amount that you pay. In some niches, Android users may have given you a higher conversion rate while lowering your cost. This is why it is a good idea for you to run a mobile device test in your niche to see whether that would lead to an improvement in your campaign results.

Tips for success

Dig through the data: Unearthing as much data about your target audience will add another dimension to your strategic arsenal as you formulate your Facebook branding options. The more information you have about your target audience, the more accurate your advertising campaign will be.

Further, knowing who your customers are and what they are motivated by will help you as an advertiser define a clearer, more qualified audience. Then, you'll be able to utilize digital channels like Facebook Ads to reach that audience and curate more traffic, engagement and, of course, increase your sales.

Famously, a marketing campaign for a well-known women's brand conducted an extensive ethnographic study for trends within women's apparel. The research team learned that numerous consumers of such clothing commonly used the term "darling" when describing their clothing. Thereafter, the company began using this term in their advertising campaigns and social media conversations to better connect with their customers. Immediately, the company saw an increase in the campaign's click-through rate on social media and many other sites online.

A useful online tool to help you segment your audience is using a data management platform (DMP). A tool such as this will give you the ability to segment your prospects and customers into clearly defined audiences. Thereafter, you can integrate this audience into your ad campaign on Facebook Ads. Consequently, by expanding your reach in this way, your advertising campaign will have more data to draw from and will more accurately reach targeted audiences on Facebook.

Adequately incorporating the relevant verbiage of your target audience into your ad content is a valuable way to relate to these users. On Facebook, there is ample opportunity to use their language, so to speak, due to the bevy of written content on their newsfeeds. However, this advantage is accompanied by the challenge of creating ad content that stands out from the high volume of content flooding users' feeds on a daily basis. Making use of online tools that reveal the specific verbiage of your audience, therefore, is very important for formulating ad content that catches the attention of your coveted niche audience base.

Clearly define your mission: It is important to have a clearly defined mission expressed in the about section of your Facebook business profile. This mission statement should properly articulate the purpose behind your business and pull together the essence of your company, which should include who you serve, why you serve them and what you do. Not only will this help get new people interested in your page, but it will also bring clarity and focus to your brand marketing that is almost guaranteed to help you to get more likes on Facebook.

When it comes to creating a successful mission statement for your Facebook page, ask yourself the following questions:

- What's your company story?
- What's your product or service?
- How do you help people?
- Who's your target market?
- What are the 3 problems you solve for your target market?
- Now, take that information & add it to the About section on your page

Once you have gone through all the trouble of creating your mission statement, don't be afraid to show it off. Share it in multiple posts and create a graphic that displays it for your page. This information is useful for new people who are looking for your page while at the same time making it clear what your brand is all about so you want it to be as readily available as possible.

Really know your audience: If you find that your posts were previously quite popular but things have since fallen off, then you may need to reevaluate what you know about your audience. This is especially important for brands that have been around for a prolonged period of time as even if this information was determined at one point if it is not regularly updated then the customers who have been with your brand for years could be very different people than who they once were.

Thus, it is worthwhile to take the time to reconsider your target audience, their desires, wants, needs, likes, dislikes, etc. You should also reconsider why it is they should choose your brand to stick with and what you can do to help them today. While all of these things likely seem relatively straightforward when you see them listed here when left to their own devices this is one area that stumps brands the most. Remember, if you spread yourself too thin when it comes to choosing a target audience you will ultimately appeal to no one.

After all, it's not like you have to guess when it comes to determining who your main Facebook audience is, you have all of this data readily available under the People tab of your Facebook Insights page. This page will tell you how many women and how many men regularly view your site as well as where they are from, what age group they are in and what their primary language happens to be. You can then use this information to tailor your future content, even more, doubling down on your most prevalent metrics.

Sharpen your competitive edge: Once you are clear on the current state of your target audience, the next thing you are going to want to focus on emphasizing are the things that sets your brand apart from the competition. Sharing the things that really make your company unique are a great way to allow Facebook fans to make educated decisions on important Facebook issues such as:

- Like your page
- Engage with you online
- Buy your product
- Hire your company

Define your business style: If you could describe your brand as a person, what qualities and characteristics would stand out to you? Would your brand be brash and bold, classic and simple, modern and sophisticated? Whatever the answer, it is

293

important that you not only know it well but can clearly and succinctly point to aspects of your Facebook page that indicate as much. People like interacting with other individuals which means that the more you make your brand feel like a person, the higher your overall level of engagement is going to be. Know your message and share it consistently in a voice and tone that resonates with your fans, rinse and repeat, it really is that simple. Nevertheless, it will go a long way when it comes to building a bond of trust between you and your fans.

Be consistent with Facebook branding: If you want people to recognize your brand on Facebook and in other facets of social media then you need to ensure that there is consistency between your Facebook profile and the rest of your online presence. A recent study found that simply by keeping all of your social media outlets fully on brand increased average engagement by nearly 20 percent.

Chapter 8: Staying on Brand on Instagram

Maximize Visual Storytelling

The previously discussed topics of defining brand voice and philosophy are so important because it is your artistic director. If your core emotional tone consists of poetic, artistic, and serious, then you are going have to put a deep Grunge filter on all of your content asap. The most important aim for your photos and images is cohesion. All of your posts need to look like they are in the same visual family.

As a rule of thumb, the brighter and more colorful content tends to up engagement rates, which may be helpful for Social Media Managers while developing their strategy. However, for aspiring influencers, it is more important to strike your tone (and pose) in the way that best represents your emotional impact.

A powerful insight, however, is that content that features a face in a photo gets 38 percent more likes than content without. This again speaks to Instagram's users' expectations and desires to interact with people on the platform. If you are running a social campaign for a new product, try to make sure a model's face is featured alongside the item. Content that includes your location also boosts engagement by a walloping 45 percent! Tagging your location is obviously a way to make friends with the Instagram algorithm and put you in front of users who want to know what is going on where you are.

No matter what, your photos need to be high-quality. Instagram is photo-run and therefore the visual standards are high. Make sure if you are shooting with a camera on a phone, that images are uploaded at least 240 dpi and if using Photoshop, quality at a maximum 80 percent. This is to save an oversized image (which won't be uploaded due to file size) but also respects that image quality has to look good on phones, tablets, laptops but does not need to be at a quality level of an HD monitor.

You will also have the option to mix up your visual content from static photos to short videos. Hyperlapse is a great app that allows stop-motion video shoots that create a dynamic effect. Layout is an app that combines photos and videos together into a single Instagram post with additional custom layouts.

A word about copyright: It is extremely important that you are cautious about copyright laws and refrain from using any image that features some form of copyright on it. If you find an image and are unsure about the copyright law behind it, refrain from using it. Using images with copyright can lead to lawsuits that are costly and that ultimately damage your business's reputation and your bottom line.

It is much safer and easier to refrain from using them at all and keeping yourself protected and professional. Any image marketed as "royalty free" means that the image does not have any copyright law attached to it that requires you to credit or pay the artist. This means that you will not have to worry about copyright infringement and you can use the image as you please. There are hundreds of thousands of stock images online, so you can easily find new ones without having to reuse old ones. Plus, more are regularly being updated to popular sites like the aforementioned ones, Pixabay and Unsplash, on a daily basis!

Tips for success

Use the idea of shout-outs to get more followers: If you want to increase your following, make sure that you are collaborating rather than competing. You need to work with the idea of share for share. The basics of this are simple. You ask someone who is an influencer in your niche if they would be willing to share some of your content. And then, in return, you will share some of their content as well.

This can be beneficial to both parties. You are able to expose each other's brands to a new audience, and some of these may be new to both of you. The best part about doing a share for share is that you are likely to find some great new followers that will help your account to grow!

Viral images: As you are working on your pictures, you may want to figure out how you can create some viral images. These are great because they will encourage your fans to share and tag their friends. You can look through some other accounts to find out what is trending in the hashtags that you want to use. Then you can create some posts that are similar but put into your own style. Then release them on your page and then ask people if they are willing to tag their friends.

Thunderclap strategy: As a business on Instagram, you may want to organize a thunderclap. This can help you get a ton of accounts that you are able to share a post of yours at the same time. This strategy is going to help you drive more traffic to your account, especially if you want to sell a product. A shout-out from many influencers in your niche will guarantee that potentially thousands of followers will see your post and then decide to follow with you.

As you can see, there are a lot of different strategies that you can choose to use. Utilizing a few of these is going to ensure that you can really start to grow out your customer base, going from 1000 to 10,000 in no time at all, and even beyond that point as well.

Create an editorial plan and an editorial calendar: Once a clear content marketing strategy has been identified, shared with all team members, we can proceed to summarize what has been decided so far within the editorial plan for the social network. It means creating a document with objectives, targets and ways of creating content within a document that becomes the guide to consistently create future content to be posted on Instagram.

These contents will be programmed and inserted into an editorial calendar. Having an editorial calendar is essential because it allows you to never run out of content, as these are decided on ahead of time, with certain deadlines and with equally certain managers.

An editorial calendar is therefore made up of specific posts, inserted into a weekly and monthly calendar, to be followed to make sure you never run out of posts. Ideally, if we believe we have enough content, we could also post on Instagram every day, which means structuring an editorial calendar that needs to have several months already covered. It is, however, desirable to have a calendar that requires posting two or three times a week.

Interact with followers and create a community: Creating a community on Instagram is very important to create a Comment Marketing activity, a strategy based on comments on photos similar to those published by your company. The use of

Instagram Bot is increasingly frequent, allowing follow-up and commenting based on who uses specific hashtags within the caption.

The problem of Comment Marketing with the Bots is that it does not lead to the real creation of the community, as a simple "Nice" or a little heart is not enough to really interact with the relevant public. For this reason, for the creation of a community, it is always better to search through the hashtags of photos in line with your brand and to comment on them manually and regularly, writing something that also leads to an answer and intrigues the user so much to push them to follow you in turn.

Tips for success

Optimize your bio correctly: Many brands spend so much time agonizing over their captions and photos that they forget to pay enough attention to their bio, or if they do think about it they quickly slap something together and move on. This is a huge mistake, however, as the bio space is representative of some seriously valuable space. It is a great way to funnel new visitors towards your current promotions or just a general call to action. Here are a few things your brand should include in its bio no matter what.

- A branded hashtag to encourage tagging and sharing
- A slogan or brief description that speaks to your brand voice
- An Instagram-specific relevant bio link pointing to your homepage or a promotion (hint: you can use a URL tracker like Bitly to further assess your Instagram traffic)

Pay attention to new stories features: Stories couldn't be hotter right now and nowhere is this more evident than on Instagram which is why the platform is taking steps to ensure that brands get on board as much as possible. This includes both ads and polls as part of stories, a clear step in a branded direction. From a brand perspective, stories are great because they can be done quickly, look mediocre and still appear on brand and within the realm of expectations for stories in general.

Create more video content: While stories are currently the king of Instagram, video isn't all that far behind. While there might be more video elsewhere, it is just as important that you create quality video content for Instagram as it is for any other social media platform. Luckily, there are a wide variety of native video apps that make recording Instagram video as easy as possible. Popular examples of this include Hyperlapse and Boomerang which both allow detailed video editing from your phone. Instagram is all about compelling visual content. Videos are a prime way to instantly step up the entertainment value of your feed.

Work on your publishing frequency: If you aren't posting your Instagram content on a schedule then you are doing your brand a marked disservice. There are clear times that posting to social media is better than others. As anything you can do to increase engagement is a huge plus, taking the times of day that people are naturally more likely to interact with this type of content is a great step in the right direction.

Studies show that people are going to be more likely to interact with your post if they can read it early in the morning when they don't yet have to worry about the stressors of the day. Posts made during this time also have less ancillary online noise to compete with, which also goes a long way towards a prospective customer taking more time to look through your offerings than they might otherwise, especially if they know you have a reputation for quality. If you take the time of day you make your posts into account, you are likely to see as much as a 20 percent increase in click-through rate.

In addition to the time of day, the same ideas apply to the days of the week you ultimately decide to post your most important content. Studies show that posts made Friday evening after 8 pm, Saturday and Sunday all have a statistically higher chance of leading to conversions with posts made Saturday gaining the biggest boost of an additional 25 percent. This occurs for the same reason as above, there simply aren't that many people taking advantage of the off-peak hours and people have more free time which makes them more likely to interact with this type of content.

Include a call to action in every caption: Much as with your bio, there is more to an Instagram caption than meets the eye. Instead of passively posting, captions are a great way to show off your brand's creativity while improving engagement at the same time. Here are a few useful calls to action to get you started:

- Asking questions
- Encourage sharing via hashtags and regrams
- Publish "tag-a-friend" posts that encourage conversations between users
- Point people to your bio link

Reconsider your use of hashtags: There are so many hashtags out there that many brands have lost sight of how to use them correctly. The two main functions of a good hashtag are to make it easy to find your posts with a basic search and to encourage your audience to share the post as well. Whatever you do, however, keep in mind that when it comes to hashtags, less is definitely more and if you use too many you will only end up making it so that your potential target audience just ignores you.

It is also important to keep up to date on the current hashtags that are trending n your niche. When you monitor hashtags that are related to your brand it is key in keeping you in the know with new posts of competitors and customers. You'll also find accounts that are interesting to follow that are vital for brand awareness.

Be aware that you could be *'shadow-banned'* for using the same hashtags for every post. This means that the posts of shadow-banned accounts don't show in the Instagram hashtag search. The account is cut off on purpose and the probability of being recommended to users will drop severely.

- Enter a hashtag you used already and do a search in Combin

- Sort the popular results

- Right-click your mouse to pick posts that are popular and look like a post you would use to your business account

- Take the cursor and hover on *Add Search* on the menu for the post

- All the hashtags that have been mentioned in the post are within the drop-down menu. Now you can use all the hashtags too and not be *shadow-banned*

Chapter 9: Staying on Brand on YouTube

Contrary to popular belief, it is not how many viewers or likes you have, or even how many existing subscribers you have on your channel. What YouTube actually pays most attention to when deciding where to place you on the search rankings is the number of watch time minutes your videos have from those who are landing on your video. In other words, if people are watching your videos all the way through, or at least are watching them longer than any other videos in your similar search terms, then you are going to get listed higher in the feed.

So, as a YouTube content creator, your primary objective aside from creating consistent and high-quality content is creating content that encourages people to actually stick around and watch your videos all the way through. The longer your videos are watched, the more your audience is going to see from you and the easier it will be for you to organically reach new audience members through the search rankings on YouTube.

The reason why YouTube favors watch times over anything else is that if your video receives a higher watch time, this must mean that your content is interesting and that people are actually enjoying watching it all. When your watch time is low, YouTube assumes that you are offering low quality or uninteresting content that is going to bore their own members and leave them unwilling to return to watch more creators in the future. Remember, YouTube grows by spotlighting their best users and giving their viewers the best and most relevant viewing experience possible. For that reason, they will always prefer people who are experiencing higher engagement and retained viewers over anyone else because this, to their algorithm, is proof that you are keeping your shared audience interested.

YouTube calculates the average viewing time by taking the total number of watched minutes on your video and dividing it by the number of people who have actually gone to your video to watch it. So, say you have 100 watch time minutes and you have had 25 unique viewers, the average watch time for your video would be 4 minutes. YouTube will then rank you lower than anyone who has experienced at 4:01 watch time or higher, and higher than anyone who has experienced a 3:59 watch time or lower.

Curate bespoke content: Video is easily the best medium for marketing online. Case studies that include client interviews, behind-the-scenes footage (especially involving things most viewers don't have access to), humorous web series or videos that tug at emotion are great places to start. At the same time, however, it is important to not try and force your brand to try and be something it's not. If your brand is about being serious and nonsense, for example, then a humorous web series might not be the right choice but a how-to video might be right up your alley. More important is keeping the channel fresh with new content and keeping the videos a reasonable length.

Don't rule out memes: Memes in their current form have become far more ubiquitous than anyone ever anticipated. While hardly the most unique or compelling way to add a bit of visual flair to your content, they are quick, easy to make and the most popular ones have a built-in degree of popularity that can make it easy for you to seem as though you have your finger on the pulse of the internet. They are also extremely easy to make thanks to the hundreds of meme generators that can easily be found online. On the other hand, however, they aren't going to be appropriate for all audiences and the meme that you choose is inherently going to leave your posted feeling dated to a current place and time. They are best used for basic content and avoided when you are creating cornerstone content which tends to be more evergreen.

Consider how-to videos

If you are already skilled in a particular area of expertise that you know others might be interested in learning more about, then there are multiple ways to take advantage of that fact and improve your brand recognition at the same time. While it will likely take you more time to create the videos you are going to use via this method than some of the others described in previous chapters, if you do it properly you can easily continue reaping the benefits from your creations for years to come.

When it comes to knowing a skill well enough to record yourself teaching that skill to another person it is important to be more than simply knowledgeable of the skill, you need to be fluent in it. This means you need to not just know how to do something but you know how to do it in the simplest and most effective way possible. If this sounds like you, then you may have what it takes to create your own series of webinars.

Before going down this road it is important to keep in mind that the type of information that people are looking for is going to be either fairly high level, filtered through a unique lens or filled with enough personality that users are willing to come to you as opposed to simply seeking out essentially the same information somewhere else on YouTube. If you think you might have what it takes but aren't quite sure, consider the following:

Play to your strengths: Many people who initially like the sound of creating a webinar quickly fall out of favor with the idea, simply because they have a limiting view in mind of just what other people are looking to learn. It is important to keep to the field related to your brand, though you can stray a little if you have something tangentially related that you happen to be extremely good at.

Express your content clearly: With a viable topic in mind, the next thing you are going to need to do is to determine the best way to express your topic in a way that makes it easy for other people to follow along with. Depending on the topic you choose, this could be something as simple as recording yourself talking about the topic while doing it or it could be more complicated and include some type of PowerPoint presentation. While the exact way you go about explaining your content doesn't matter, it is important that the visual and audio quality is professional, after all, you want to come off as an expert in the field, not someone who is trying to make extra money off of a YouTube video recorded on their phone.

Market your content: Once you have a page that is full of videos, the next thing you will want to do is get the word out about your webinar. Besides spreading the word via social media and encourage all of your friends and family to do the same; you never know when something might go viral and word of mouth is enough to boost the sales of a webinar significantly if it gets in front of the right people.

With that out of the way, the next thing you will want to do is visit websites that the people in your chosen niche are likely to congregate around. Once you find these sites you are going to want to spend time in their forums, answering questions that people pose about the topics. Every time you do so, you are then going to want to credit your YouTube page as the place you found the information. With enough posts all carrying your website, you can be sure that word will start to spread and you will start to see additional hits on your page as a result.

Chapter 10: Find a Mentor

Learning from someone who is older, wiser, and has been there before is an obvious and invaluable opportunity regardless if you are just getting started marketing your brand or if you have been struggling along for years. Working on your brand day in and day out can make it very easy to get so focused on the trees that you don't see the forest, a mentor has the ability to step in and see things from a very different perspective.

While most people would agree that a mentor is a great thing to have, nearly all of them would be at a loss when it comes to actually finding one. In order to get started finding your perfect mentor, there are a few things you can do.

Define what you are looking for: In order to find a mentor that is going to provide you with everything you need, the first thing you are going to need to consider is what you are looking for from your career as well as the relationship in general. This could well involve goals that you need to take on personally, such as becoming more knowledgeable in the field, before you can move forward. After all, you need to be considered a catch as well if you want to attract a quality mentor.

You also need to keep in mind that you will need to treat the start of a potential mentor relationship like any other business friendship which means it needs to be taken slow. Be friendly and casual and avoid outright asking if they will be your mentor in the first five minutes. The best place to meet potential mentors is via your existing professional network, especially if you work or in contact with people who may provide you with a little advice from time to time already.

Even when you are dedicated to the idea of finding a mentor, it is important to focus an equal or greater amount of energy on developing a personal reputation for success, you never know when a mentor might seek you out. What's more, by placing the focus on your own career you are naturally setting yourself up to meet veterans in your industry who will want to help you to nurture the talent they see in you.

The fact of the matter is that many talented people are always on the lookout for younger individuals with the skills and talent they need for one project or another, believe it or not, these types of people are often in short supply. Even if you aren't actively looking for a mentor at the moment, developing a reputation as someone who is well-balanced, reliable, motivated and talent will have potential mentors sniffing around.

Understand the relationship: While keeping the first step in mind, it is also very important to understand the average mentor/mentee relationship so that you can set your expectations accordingly. First and foremost, this means that it is rare that the relationship is a formal, official, thing and you can learn just as much from a standard professional relationship with someone who is willing to show you the ropes as you can from someone who feels the need to actually use the word mentor.

What's more, these relationships rarely take the form of a short, intensive, one-on-one scenario and instead tend to more often take the form of a long-form dialogue with the more experienced party helping to teach and spark inspiration in the less experienced party. As such, it is unreasonable to expect that just finding a mentor is going to change your life completely overnight.

Part of finding a mentor is about learning how to add value to the career and value of your mentor, while at the same time being proactive with your personal career growth. These types of lessons apply to workers at any stage of their career but are especially important for those with less experience to keep in mind if they hope to be successful. Sometimes, all you need in these moments is someone to look up to, someone who has been in your shoes but created their own path to success.

Finding your mentor

Qualities of a good mentor: First and foremost, it is important to understand that every mentor is different and finding one you are on the same page as is far more important than finding the "best" option based on some arbitrary metric. Though, at the very least they should have a track record of success and more experience at you in your chosen niche.

It is important to look for a mentor who has the character and traits you want to emulate if you don't have to pick and choose which aspects of your mentor to follow. On the other hand, some great mentors may help you to learn who not to be like – for example, a very successful businessman who is struggling in his personal life. Great mentors have a complementary skill set and bring different qualities to the table. Different perspectives are valuable in the mentor-mentee relationship.

Important character traits to look out for include things like honesty, creativity, empathy, and authenticity. Honesty is especially important as you want someone who will be able to give you constructive criticism or a reality check when you need it, but empathy is also important because it is important to know when you need encouragement as well. It is also important that you share the same values when it comes to management and leadership as otherwise, you are likely to get far less out of the experience than you otherwise would.

Make a five-year plan: When it comes to finding your mentor, the first thing you are going to want to consider is your five-year plan and what you want out of your career in that time. You should leave some room for uncertainty, certainly, but defining what you want in the short-term can make it easier for you to determine how you should move forward. This will help you to determine who currently has your dream job, which is a great place to start when it comes to finding an ideal mentor.

If you can 't find an exact match then you will want to work to find someone who can provide advice about your industry and has a good idea of what it takes to advance from where you are to where you want to be. A person with a better idea of your current role and what it takes to move on from there will be able to give you more relevant advice when it comes to things like potential projects to explore or types of training you need to get ahead.

Making contact: After you have put your sights on someone specific, the next thing you will want to do is reach out in an appropriate fashion. It is important to keep things casual for as long as your potential mentor is comfortable with, remember this relationship will develop over time. Very few people want to be around someone who is overeager all of the time, don't try and force things and understand that advice and lessons will happen organically over time.

Likewise, it is important to not be so anxious that you overstep basic social graces. Keep the following in mind to ensure you don't come off as awkward. Communication involves verbal and nonverbal interactions. Nonverbal communication is what we display through our body language; such as our facial expressions, giving eye contact, hand gestures, and our body posture. Nonverbal communication helps by offering reinforcement, insight into someone's emotional status, provide feedback and help conversation flow. Utilizing nonverbal communication is easier to learn than interpreting someone else's nonverbal gestures and cues.

Your physical stance or posture during a conversation conveys messages to the person you are trying to communicate with. The distance you stand from someone can show someone how you feel about them. A closer distance is more personal and usually used with people you have established a close relationship with or you are hoping to establish a closer relationship with. Your posture can demonstrate how you feel about the person or conversation; such as if you are folding your arms you can look intimidating to others and if you are slouching you may be perceived as not interested.

When first starting a conversation with a new potential mentor, it is important to send them subconscious signals which say you are open to the conversation you are having and to their presence in general. Keep your arms and legs from crossing. and try to smile naturally, but not a full smile, in an inviting manner. You don't need to maintain eye contact exclusively, but you should be directly involved with the other person at all times. Avoid the temptation to look at your phone as a way to fill silences and instead actively engage in conversation

Eye contact shows someone you are interested in what they are saying and that you are truly listening. People will pay close attention to someone's facial expressions and use them as a way to determine how someone is feeling.

An upright, attentive positive with your hands on your knees which are spread a moderate degree will show the person you are speaking with that you are energetic and ready to learn. Leaning forward a little in this position will likewise show that you are engaged in the conversation and eager to hear more. Make a point of keeping your shoulders straight, but not tense, as that tension will be easily visible to your potential mentor.

On the other hand, sitting back in your chair with one leg crossed over the other (at the knee, crossing at the ankles will make you look too relaxed) will put you in more of a confident and commanding position. This position says that you are confident in your abilities and with how the conversation is going in general. Sitting forward says you are eager, sitting back says you are experienced. If you do sit back it is important to keep an extra focus on eye contact, this will convey you are still connected to what the other person is saying.

Many mentees make the mistake of assuming that during the early part of mentorship they will be learning earth-shattering secrets all of the time. The fact of the matter is that you often can't force a learning situation which means you need to be available for them when they come. Likewise, without the benefit of the mentor's experience, it can be hard to tell what is a learning moment while it is occurring so it is best to always keep an open mind.

Strengthening your mentor relationship: Once you've met someone you would like to be your mentor and have successfully stuck up an initial conversation, the next step is following up in such a way that the relationship can blossom from there. If it appears that they are going to be interested in continuing a dialog you will want to set a calendar reminder to follow up at the right time. The frequency with which you speak with your mentor is ultimately up to you, but it is important that the goal should be continued insight into the long-term.

This could mean hopping on the phone or meeting for coffee once a quarter, or even just twice a year. While in-person meetings are important, social media offers mentees the opportunity to have regular, no-pressure interactions with mentors. Use Twitter and LinkedIn for light things – interesting articles, book recommendations, important industry news, etc.

Social media provides an easy way for a mentee to reach out to the mentor in a nonconfrontational or needy way while also showing that they value the relationship that is being created at the same time. It is still important to avoid overdoing it, however, because at this stage it is still very easy to come off as pushy; remember, you want the relationship to form is as casual a way as possible. Likewise, it is important to avoid discussing the important stuff via social media as this will make the need for face-to-face interaction lessen even more. If their schedule is really that full, then even a Skype call is better than simply emailing back and forth constantly.

Finally, it is important to not underestimate snail mail in this scenario. Taking the time to send a handwritten thank-you note or holiday card will show that you are willing to go above and beyond the norm for the relationship and is far more likely to stick in your potential mentor's mind than an email saying the same thing.

Adding value to the relationship: As the mentee, it can be easy to end up in a situation where you are constantly asking for things without giving anything back. While many mentors will be happy to continue dishing out advice free of charge, it would likely be far easier to get a hold of them if they got something out of the experience besides whatever pleasure they get from helping out the younger generation.

While you might not be in a position to much for them at the moment, at the very least you are going to want to show that you appreciate all they do for you, and always be on the lookout for other ways to show your appreciation in a more tangible way as well. At the very least this should translate into a clear appreciation of your mentor's time by arriving at meetings early and working around your mentor's schedule as much as possible.

Chapter 11: Keep Tabs on Your Brand

Utilizing Facebook AdManager

Once your campaign has begun and you are delivering ads to your pre-selected target audience, you need to know whether or not those ads are having the impact you are seeking on the audience you selected, and *why* they are having that impact.

You need to know:

- The demographics you are reaching.
- The types of devices that have been used to view your ad.
- How many unique people you have reached across various platforms.

With people-based metrics across multiple platforms, Facebook Ads Manager can help businesses fill in these blanks. All of this information is easily accessible within the Facebook Ads Manager, allowing you to tailor your ads to your needs, to your audience, and to your budget. This is a highly customizable experience, and the simple, easy-to-use interface makes the Facebook Ads Manager ideal for those without experience advertising, and those trying to start or grow a new business.

With the Ad Performance tools built into the Facebook Ads Manager, you can quickly learn which ads your audience prefers, which products or services they are most interested, and who your true target demographic is. Facebook Ads Manager will give you every tool you need to successfully market your business, brand or product, all on your own!

Ads Manager Overview

The following is a list of terms you will need to know to use Ads Manager effectively:

- *Delivery:* This refers to your ad campaigns, ad sets, and ads and their overall status. This determines how your ad is seen by your target audience.

- *Results:* This refers to the objectives you defined when you initially set up your ad campaign. For example, if you selected Page Views as your objective, the Results column will show you how many times your page has been viewed.

- *Reach vs. Impressions*: Reach is the number of people who have seen your ad at least once. Reach is different from "Impressions," in that Impressions include people who have seen your ad multiple times. They refer to those audience members as "Impressions," because your ad obviously left an impression on them for them to view it more than once.

- *Cost per results:* This is the average amount your ad costs per result. It is calculated by dividing the amount spent by the amount in the Results column. For example, if your company spent $100 on a conversion campaign, and your ad netted 50 conversions, then the cost per result would amount to $2. Therefore, you paid $2 for each view your ad received.

- *Amount spent*: This is the total amount your company has spent on ads, ad sets, and campaigns. It always shows the last 30 days by default. As mentioned

317

previously, Facebook Ads Manager bills you on a monthly basis - you do not have to pay for the entire ad campaign at once. This is incredibly beneficial to those with small budgets or those that are new to advertising, that may need to adjust their budgets as time goes on.

- *Ends:* This is the date your campaign is scheduled to end. This date is chosen when the ad campaign is initially scheduled and published. This end date is not set in stone, however, and you can add time to any ad campaign that you want with a few simple clicks. However - keep in mind that extending your campaign will alter your budget. If you do not increase your budget at the same time that you extend your ad campaign, then less of your budget will be spent per day, to make up for that extension. Extending an ad campaign is only wise if you can increase your budget, as well.

Using Reporting Controls within Facebook Ads Manager

Reporting controls are used to locate specific campaigns, to find out which ads are performing well, and which ones need to be turned off or altered. You can use the following options to find the information that you may be looking for:

- Search
  - This will allow you to customize a report based on keywords and responses. This is especially helpful if you are trying to locate a specific reaction(s) from your audience. Try organizing your report by searching for keywords like love, great, awesome.

318

- You can also use negative keywords to identify campaigns that are having a less positive response. Try organizing your report by searching for keywords like expensive, scam, poor.
- Date Range
  - This will allow you to arrange a report that details your ad campaigns in any date range that you choose. This can help you identify trends that your business may experience with advertising - if there are certain months that are busier or more profitable than others.
- Breakdown
  - The breakdown feature gives you an incredibly detailed report and a wealth of information. You may want to use this report control in conjunction with the report filters, that way you are not overwhelmed with information.
- Filters
  - These filters make the Facebook reports exceptionally customizable, allowing you to remove or add any data field that you want to create a report that will detail exactly what you need to know.
- Columns
  - You can arrange these columns in whatever organizational method you choose - especially if you intend to export your reports to Microsoft Excel.

Using these parameters can help you identify which demographics are most successful if there was a certain period of time that your ad campaign saw the most traction. Study these reports closely; there is no limit to what you can learn about your ad campaign from them!

Analyzing your results

The following list will help you to understand the significance of the various results you may find in the Facebook Ads Manager report generator.

- *Brand Awareness:* This provides an estimation as to the number of people who may remember your ads within a two-day period. This result is significant if you have objectives such as Video Views, Engagement, Brand Awareness, and Post Engagement. The reason they chose to a two day period is simply that studies show that if you recall seeing an ad two days after you initially saw it, you are significantly more likely to recall the name of the product or business a week or even a month later.

- *Reach vs. Impressions:* Reach is the number of people who have seen your ad at least one time. Reach is different from Impressions in that Impressions include people who have seen your ad multiple times, whether because they seek it out repeatedly or because it appears in their News Feed repeatedly.

- *Traffic:* This provides the number of actions your ads have contributed to your mobile app, and therefore recorded as "app events." This also provides the number of clicks your ads have received on the desktop and mobile devices, which allows you to track how many people have used your ad to access your website - or whatever other clickable content has been attached.

- *Engagement:* This provides the total number of actions your ads have stimulated. This includes Facebook page "Likes" from ad engagement, the number of people that marked themselves as "Interested" or "Going To" an event your company has organized and streaming reactions from live broadcasts. This information is vital when determining whether or not your ad campaign has been successful.

- *App Installs:* This provides the total number of "app events." By "app events," we are referring to the installation of your app or the uninstallation of your app. This records how effectively your ads are contributing to the success of your mobile application.

- *Video Views:* This provides the number of views your video ads have received. The view is only counted if it has lasted for an aggregate of three seconds or more. It also indicates how many times your videos have been watched to completion.

- *Lead Generation:* This provides the number of forms your customers have filled out online, as a result of Facebook lead ads.

- *Messages:* This provides the number of Facebook Messenger messages exchanged between your company and your customers.

- *Conversions:* Conversions are chosen at the ad set level. This may include "Add to Cart," "Initiate Checkout," and "Make Purchase," if your goal is to obtain direct product sales from your ad campaign.

- *Catalog Sales:* This provides the number of sales recorded at your stores as a result of Facebook ads, as recorded by Facebook Pixel.

- *Store Visits:* This provides the number of people who have visited your store or stores after seeing your ads on Facebook.

Scheduling and Sharing Reports

The following list will help you to understand the various actions available in the Reports section of the Facebook Ads Manager.

- *Schedule:* You can schedule reports to send automatically to anyone that has access to the account. This can be done on a daily, weekly, or even monthly basis, and you can maintain as many as a thousand reports in your ad account.

- *Export:* You can also export reports or advertising data directly into Microsoft Excel, using the free Excel Add-on available in Facebook Ads Manager.

- *Share:* If you do not send or export the reports, you can also create a clickable link to the Ad Manager and you can share that link.

- *Download:* Finally, you can download reports as .csv or .xls files. These reports can then be copied to a USB drive, attached to an email, sent via instant messenger, or shared in any other way possible.

In addition, the Microsoft Office Store offers a plugin with Facebook Ads Manager, which allows you to download ad account directly into Excel. With this plug-in, you can:

- Download performance data using reporting controls - like filters - so that you can create custom reports in Ads Manager.
- Create custom templates that allow you to run reports quickly.
- Refresh the data as often as necessary.
- Use Excel's pivot tables and other tools to generate a custom analysis of ad performance.

The Excel plug-in is just as user-friendly and customizable as the Facebook Ad Manager, allowing you to create report templates that are based entirely on the metrics most important to you and your business.

Email marketing

Another way you can be sure to keep tabs on your target audience is by making an effort to collect reader emails and then email them using something called an autoresponder to send them new links to products you are promoting automatically once the information has been collected. Consider the following tips to create the type of autoresponder messages that get the response you need to start seeing real results in the long term:

Choose the right products: When setting up an autoresponder message, you will want to pick an average of 5 products that do not directly compete with one another but are still clearly related.

Track your data: In addition to sending out a new unsolicited email every 4 days, you need to track the emails that you do send out and determine how many people opened each email and how many actually bought something because of it. As you gain more information to work off of you can more specifically target your emails to have a better success rate among your target audience.

Understand open rate: When it comes to understanding what you can do to ensure that your autoresponder emails are opened, the first thing you will want to do is to send emails from your name directly. Assuming you have connected your name with your brand, opening an email from you should be akin to opening an email from anyone else your readers know. Outside of that, there are several important guidelines to consider to ensure readers keep opening your unsolicited emails for years to come.

- *Create the right subject line:* 35 percent of your subscribers will open any email with the right subject line. This means your subject line should be short and sweet, no more than 10 words but no fewer than 6. The subject line should imply useful content related to the niche in question. This ensures you are at least including something you know your audience should, in theory, be interested in.

- *Find the right topic:* When it comes to finding useful content that you know your audience is interested in, the best place to start is with the posts that have gotten the greatest number of views previously and expand on that information.

- *Follow through:* If you expect your subscribers to open content that they know is going to try and sell them something you must deliver on your promise for quality useful content every single time.

- *Be conversational:* The last thing that any of your

subscribers are going to want to read is some copy that reads like a sales pitch right from the beginning. You will find much more success if you write your emails in the same way you would compose an email to a friend, just with likely significantly more comment before you get to the reason you are actually emailing (the 5 ad links at the bottom of the email).

- *Contrast Pain and Gain:* When it comes to defining the pain in your current email, you need to ask yourself what you are focusing on that your subscribers are interested in and focus on how they can gain the ability to mitigate that pain through one of the items that you are so thoughtfully providing links to.

Regardless of what strategy you choose to pursue, the majority of all affiliate marketers proceed using one of three main autoresponders who all offer similar features and the ability to create numerous autoresponder series and send them out automatically when certain conditions are met.

Mistakes to avoid:

1. *Giving up to soon:* Even with a decent amount of coaching it can still be quite difficult to find the right niche, the right platform, the right affiliates, and the right website. While certain things about affiliate marketing will only improve with time when you are starting out it is important to not necessarily worry about doing everything perfectly right from the start and to persevere when things go pear-shaped.

2. *Spreading yourself too thin:* When you are first starting out it can be easy to feel desperate to get new followers

anyway you can, whether it is above board or not. This is a mistake, however, as you can easily find yourself in a position where you are trying to sell an inferior product to a market that isn't interested. While it may be scary to turn down an affiliate at first, you will end up with a stronger portfolio of marketing opportunities in the long run if you get comfortable with waiting for the right offer to come along.

3. *Not putting enough time into your content:* Not everyone is naturally suited to regularly generating content seven days a week, and that is perfectly alright, if you don't look for alternatives for content generation, however, you will never get your new accounts off of the ground. Whether it means putting more time in yourself until you get it right, or paying someone else to do it for you, the quality of your content should always be as high as possible.

4. *Focusing too much on keywords:* While having the right keywords in the right places will certainly help, you should be more focused on providing high quality, on niche, content and let the rankings take care of themselves. Keywords were king for a long time, but that time has passed, focus on creating the most unique value for readers that you can and your ranking will improve as a result.

5. *Not doing your research:* It is important to remember that your website is your most important asset when it comes to making money via affiliate marketing in the long term which means not letting any subpar products onto your pages. This means researching every product before you take on an affiliate role. If your regular

readers trust you and buy into a bad product that trust is never going to be rebuilt.

6. *Not keeping track of sales:* When you receive commissions from merchants, they won't tell you what it is for precisely, that is up to you to track on your own. It is important to do so to determine what your readers are into specifically, not based on their niche. This is easily taken care of, however, as most merchants will provide you with the ability to create unique identification numbers to each of your links to determine what went where.

7. *Pushing too hard:* While it is your job to convince people to visit the merchant's site with the intent to buy something, it is not your job to sell the product. You should make it a point of describing the strengths and weakness of products in a way that appears unbiased, if a little leading, anything more aggressive is a surefire way to turn readers off of your site for good.

8. *Worrying too much about the money:* It is important to start off down the path of the affiliate marketer with the appropriate expectations in place. This means that it will take a while for your readership to grow and for your affiliate connections to starting bearing fruit. It is important to not expect too much too soon as this can cause you to give up, possibly before you finally saw the big turnaround you have been expecting.

9. *Being too enthusiastic:* When you are first starting out it can be difficult to hold back your enthusiasm for the items you are marketing, after all, if other people buy them then you see a profit. This can lead many affiliate

marketers to inflate the claims of the products they are promoting which is never recommended. While it will likely lead to an increase in the number of units of that item that are sold in the short-term it will hurt your long term sales potential.

10. *Discounting the importance of building a user list:* While you may not be at a point where an autoresponder makes sense just yet, your goal should be to do everything in your power to be prepared when that day comes which means taking advantage of all of your early adopters and putting together an email list as soon as possible. Even if you aren't planning on using it right away, the point where a reader first accesses your site is one of the best times to get their information, don't waste it.

11. *Focusing on a single source of visitors:* Especially when you first build your site, you are going to want to do everything you can to ensure you are driving traffic to it from as many places as possible. This is especially vital early on as otherwise, your ranking will never rise to where it needs to be to see the types of long term, reliable results you are hoping for.

12. *Moving between affiliate programs too quickly:* It is important to fully finish working on whatever ideas you have in regards to a particular affiliate offer before moving on to the next. While you will eventually be able to multitask, early on you will have little experience to judge the amount of time a project will take which means what seems like a simple second program can spin out of control quickly. Do yourself a favor and take it slow until you have a firm idea of what to expect moving forward.

13. *Branching out too soon:* While new and exciting niches may come your way on a regular basis it is important to hold off from creating a second site dedicated to a different niche before you have fully gotten the first off of the ground.

14. *Not doing market research:* If you do not invest in Audience Research upfront then you are doomed to fail. If you place a good ad in front of people who are not interested, then you are basically wasting money. With the diverse audience that is on Facebook, you could be talking to a small, large or even larger audience than you know. Targeting the wrong group with the wrong ad is not going to provide you with any benefits. So, run some tests for your audience, find out what they like and don't like. Make sure your ads are going to attract the clientele you are hoping for.

    a. Ask yourself, "Would I be willing to bet money on them liking this ad?" if the answer is no then it's not the right ad. Also choose a niche product, marketing to the whole is not going to be as easy as most people think. If you niche it down, you can talk to that niche much easier and draw in more sales.

15. Place yourself in the customer's shoes. Then ask these questions:

    - What would they be Googling?
    - What pages on Facebook would they be liking?
    - Who is there influencers or celebrity crushes?
    - What type of apps are they using?

- Which magazines or blogs are they reading right now?
- Who are they already buying form that is a competitor?
- Where are they hanging out on Reddit?

Find out what differentiates them from all the other people out there. If you locate a Facebook page that you come across in your research, then go and check it out. Like the page and follow some of the trends and posts. Facebook will also offer some related pages and groups to follow and this will give you insight into other aspects of the niche. If they do not have a strong connection to being buyers or product users don't follow them. By using Facebooks audience insight tools you can brainstorm much easier the targeting concepts behind the interests and qualities that make your potential clients feel good. You can gain insight into behaviors and much more.

Conclusion

Thanks for making it through to the end of *Social Media Marketing 2019: How to Brand Yourself Online Through Facebook, Twitter, YouTube & Instagram - Highly Effective Strategies for Digital Networking, Personal Branding, and Online Influence*, let's hope it was informative and able to provide you with all of the tools you need to achieve your goals. Just because you've finished this book doesn't mean there is nothing left to learn on the topic, and expanding your horizons is the only way to find the mastery you seek.

Now that you have made it to the end of this book, you hopefully have an understanding of how to get started improving your brand through the use of social media, as well as a strategy or two, or three, that you are anxious to try for the first time. Before you go ahead and start giving it your all, however, it is important that you have realistic expectations as to the level of success you should expect in the near future.

While it is perfectly true that some people experience serious success right out of the gate, it is an unfortunate fact of life that they are the exception rather than the rule. What this means is that you should expect to experience something of a learning curve, especially when you are first figuring out what works for you. This is perfectly normal, however, and if you persevere you will come out the other side better because of it. Instead of getting your hopes up to an unrealistic degree, you should think of your time spent strengthening your brand as a marathon rather than a sprint which means that slow and steady will win the race every single time.

Finally, if you found this book useful in any way, a review on Amazon is always appreciated!

Made in the USA
Monee, IL
16 September 2019